Charles Seale-Hayne Library
University of Plymouth
(01752) 588 588
LibraryandITenquiries@plymouth.ac.uk

Shipping Policy in the European Community

PAUL HART
GILLIAN LEDGER
MICHAEL ROE
BRIAN SMITH
Institute of Marine Studies, University of Plymouth

Avebury

Aldershot · Brookfield USA · Hong Kong · Singapore · Sydney

Published by
Avebury
Ashgate Publishing Limited
Gower House
Croft Road
Aldershot
Hants GU11 3HR
England

Ashgate Publishing Company
Old Post Road
Brookfield
Vermont 05036
USA

A CIP catalogue record for this book is available from the British Library and the US Library of Congress.

ISBN 1 85628 348 8

Printed and Bound in Great Britain by
Athenaeum Press Ltd, Newcastle upon Tyne.

Contents

Acknowledgements

With thanks from:

Gillian   -   to Alan and Janette, for their support, and to Liam for his patience.

Brian   -   to his mother and father, for all the sacrifices they made, and to Alison for all her help and encouragement.

Paul   .   -   to the multitudes who helped on the way.

Michael   -   to Sue Blackman, for all the toil and sweat and to the four Cantons.

> 'But now you're here
> I feel no fear.
> I can't believe
> The news from Heaven.
> You close your eyes
> On a World inside.
> A spark of life
> On a wire from Heaven.'

Preface

Michael Roe

The three papers presented in this volume emerged from a period of intense research activity in the Institute of Marine Studies, at the University of Plymouth centring on work looking at the development of European Community maritime policy between 1988 and 1991.

Unlike many other sectors of interest for the European Community, the maritime field had been sadly neglected for many years in terms of legislation and policy. One immediate consequence of the 1987 Single European Act and its requirement for the establishment of a single European market by 1 January 1993 was the need for legislation to create a harmonized and liberalized maritime market. Hence, this research activity.

No attempt is made in this volume to provide a comprehensive review of all maritime issues - that would require a far longer text and one that would take far longer to produce and in the context of a constantly changing legislative environment, one that would be outdated before it was published. However, the contributions enclosed here do provide a commentary on three very significant maritime areas.

Gillian Ledger's paper represents a detailed analysis of the relationship between the United Kingdom and the European Community in the shipping sector, and highlights the contrasts between policies emerging, paradoxically, from the same objective of achieving a liberalized maritime market. Paul Hart's individual contribution is in linking the shipping and ship building industries of the European Community in an analysis of state subsidy. Meanwhile, that of Brian Smith provides a detailed analysis of the EUROS proposals for a flag for the European Community and is particularly relevant at a time when revised proposals are currently (early 1992) under discussion.

All three research projects have emerged from the maritime business area of the Institute of Marine Studies which specialises in studies of maritime economies, policy, law, operations and planning.

Without the dedication, enthusiasm and energy of the three individuals involved this

1

text would never have emerged. They each contributed to an enjoyable and stimulating atmosphere, and one for which I, amongst others, will be eternally grateful.

Michael Roe,
Buckland Monachorum, Devon
10 April 1992.

1 Introduction

Michael Roe

The main objectives of the opening paper by Gillian Ledger can be outlined as:

1. To assess the shipping policies of the United Kingdom (UK) and the European Community (EC).

2. To obtain an assessment of the relative success or failure in policy formulation of each, with respect to shipping.

3. To identify the problems that any conflict between the UK and EC policies may present.

4. To suggest ways forward for the future in terms of UK and EC maritime policy making.

It is widely believed that the shipping policies of the European Community and the UK differ markedly in style and approach. These contrasts in policy and the conflict they suggest help to indicate consequential existing problems for the maritime industry and to suggest possible solutions to them.

The issue involved is a topical one and makes the analysis both worthwhile and significant. The maritime sector has notable influences on major issues such as international and national trade and economics and defence. This is made more significant by the well reported decline in the UK shipping fleet - both in real terms and in relation to the rest of the EC, (Commission of the European Communities, 1989) and that of the EC shipping fleet as a whole (European Community Ship Owners Association, 1989) and is brought into even more prominence by the differences known to exist in state aid provided by the individual nation states of the European Community. The topicality of the work is made more significant by the continuing attempts by the EC to formulate a maritime policy during 1990 and 1991.

The Single European Act (1987) and its deadline for completion of a Single European Market places an increasing requirement for Community members to have compatible and harmonized policies in all fields and this includes that of the maritime sector.

Previous work in the area of European maritime policies is surprisingly limited with only Erdmenger and Stasinopoulos (1988), Bredimas (1981), Bray (1988), Middleton (1989), Steele (1986) and Tzounas (1981) having studied the issue in any real depth in recent years, along with a series of now rather outdated EC surveys and reviews of the need for a European framework for the maritime industries (Commission for the European Communities 1985). The research outlined here thus helps to contribute to the debate that will ensue up to and beyond the deadline for completion of the Single European Market.

The paper by Paul Hart represents an attempt to take a number of case studies from the European Community area and to analyze the relationship between shipping and shipbuilding state aid, and their effectiveness in supporting the maritime industries. Central to the study is an assessment of the United Kingdom's position, but interesting comparisons are drawn from Germany, the Netherlands, France and Belgium - and extensive use is made of the opinion of the United Kingdom maritime industry and its views on state aid throughout the EC.

The issue of state aid to maritime industries has been a controversial policy area of late; international conflict and intranational recession have highlighted the role of the merchant navy in contributing to a nation's economy and security.

Nowhere is this more true than in the United Kingdom; in the last decade it has been involved in two wars and experienced a number of economic problems. This has had severe implications on a merchant fleet that has experienced a substantial decline in recent years; a number of sources have expressed concern that the fleet is now incapable of supporting another Falklands ware and cite the Gulf crisis as an example of a growing dependence on support from other nations (particularly through the chartering of foreign vessels). There have also been strategic and economic implications on the employment both of seafarers and shore personnel in shipbuilding and support services.

For the UK merchant navy to contribute strategically it must prosper economically, something it is finding difficult in the light of current cost competition from abroad. It is not clear how artificial this competition is since many other nations receive varying levels of state aid especially through subsidies, seen as undesirable in traditional economic theory.

This provides a classic dilemma: should (economic) nature be allowed to take its course despite the aforementioned implications or should interventionalist action be taken, in the national interest and through subsidies to influence operating conditions.

The final paper by Brian Smith introduces the concept of open registries and the response of the European Community to the whole issue of flagging out. Although a very specific maritime issue, it is one that illustrates clearly some of the problems facing the EC in resolving the conflict between protecting their own fleets from outside 'unfair' competition, and following the basic principles of the Treaty of Rome, in encouraging free market principles wherever and whenever possible. The whole idea of a community register of shipping continues to be debated at the time of writing, but until the benefits it affords matches those of the competing open registries, or at least offshore and international registries, it appears to be destined to failure, or to very limited success.

4

2 Maritime policy in the European Community and the United Kingdom: Contrasts and conflicts

Gillian Ledger

Introduction

It is important for those engaged in the maritime industry to have knowledge of the policy framework within which maritime transport is carried out. The interests of shippers are influenced by national and international shipping policies which shippers' councils are increasingly trying to influence, to their advantage. Although general shipping policy trends have remained stable for over a decade, minor adjustments and shifts take place all the time.

Shipping is a complex industry; most of its activities are concerned with international trade involving shipping companies and shippers from various countries, international agreements and understandings, and policies of Governments. Hence, shipping policy cannot be confined to a national framework, but must take into account the international character of the industry.

Policy making is usually a continuous round of discussing objectives and problems and drafting and evaluating policies. Policies may then be approved for implementation raising questions of what methods to use and where, when and how to implement them. Technological developments and research results plus changing political contexts may mean policy modification.

Trends in contemporary shipping policy indicate that shippers' interests are being taken into account more seriously than before, evident both at the commercial and governmental levels. We can now examine a broad categorisation of maritime policies as outlined by the United Nations (1988).

Basic categories of shipping policy

a) Freedom of the seas

This suggests 'rational' treatment of foreign shipping and no Government intervention in the international shipping markets. This implies free competition in the shipping industry, with the aims of simplifying international trade and encouraging trade expansion. It also allows each country to concentrate on producing those goods and services which it could produce at lower costs than other countries, leading to optimal utilisation of the world's resources.

This freedom enabled some countries to develop large, competitive national fleets serving work markets, whilst other countries left transport of their trade to foreign shipping companies with more advantageous services.

The legal framework of this principle is found in the 'Code of Liberalization' of the OECD countries. Main elements applying to member countries are:

1. No legislation favouring national flag vessels, and no allocation of state cargo to state ships.

2. No treaty/agreement with any other country encouraging similar procedures abroad.

3. No introduction of import/export regulations, currency exchange rules or other means which influence the choice of nationality of the carrying ship.

b) Anti-trust policies

Through these, governments intervene by reducing the freedom to preserve benefits which free competition is considered to give the public in general. Hence, arguments against freedom of the seas are arguments for anti-trust policies. Counter arguments to survival of the fittest include strategic, economic and political considerations.

Also there is the possibility of one ship owner attaining a monopoly position in a particular trade, in a free market. Anti-trust policies in this case, may involve breaking up the monopoly by direct orders from the government, or encouraging others willing to compete. Alternatively, the activities of the monopolist might be controlled by controlling freight rates or other items.

On the other hand, a conference agreement may be entered into between several carriers operating on one trade, regarding transport terms. This involves constraints on competition between conference members and agreements as regards attitude to non conference shipowners. Agreements of this type may be declared illegal by the Government, or its activities may be constrained by controlling tariff schedules; or a combination of the two may be used.

Another possible situation concerns loyalty arrangements. The conference may attempt to maintain the shipper's loyalty by offering deferred rebates or dual rates. In the first example, the shipper using conference ships receives a rebate when a set time period has elapsed since the shipment, provided he has not shipped any goods with non-conference ships in that time. In the second example, two carrier tariffs exist, although the lower one is only offered to the shipper who remains loyal to the conference ships. These arrangements may be subject to governmental control through an anti-trust policy - the best example probably coming from United States Anti Trust Laws on Conferences.

c) Protectionism in shipping

This is at the other end of the spectrum to free trade and prevents shipowners from being exposed to market forces. Governments may provide protection in a number of ways:

Subsidies

Economic maritime aid may be provided to reduce the shipowner's total costs of operating a national flag vessel, the aim being to maintain or develop a national fleet.

Such support is carried out through direct or indirect assistance programmes, which are usually also a support to the national shipbuilding industry. Types of subsidy or maritime aid can be divided into three main areas:

i) Investment finance assistance includes the provision of low interest loans, interest subsidies and loan guarantees, which reduce final costs of shipping investments.

Programmes may also include longer repayment schedules and grace periods on interests and amortization.

Main investment finance assistance types are (Odeke 1988)

- Low interest loans - these loans may be provided by the government at interest rates lower than those available commercially.
- Interest subsidies - in this case the government provides assistance by paying a percentage of the interest requirements on shipping loans.
- Loan guarantees.
- Extended grace periods - this involves extending the pay back periods of loans.

These reduce capital costs of contracting and operating the vessel and are mainly aimed at promoting construction of new vessels by the national shipyard.

ii) Tax allowance programmes These are mostly indirect aids, in the form of depreciation allowances and tax free reserves, the former being the right to make larger deductions than usual from gross earnings, to improve net income after tax. The latter is the right to set aside, tax free, some gross earnings to meet future investments. Programmes also include tax exemptions, tax credits, low tax rates and reimbursement of some tax. Hence the shipping company retains a higher amount of its income in the company and builds up reserves for future activities.

The most important tax allowances are (Odeke 1988):

- Accelerated depreciation allowances.
- Tax free revenues - the company can retain a certain amount of its revenue within the company, tax free.
- Tax credits.

iii) Direct Subsidies These are of three main types:

a) Investment grants - for example, cash investment grants from the government for a percentage of cost of acquiring ships to be registered under its national flag.

b) Construction subsidies are given when a vessel is constructed at a national shipyard. Such subsidies, given to the yard, lower vessel prices.

c) Operational subsidies lower shipowners' operating costs, in order to place operations of a national vessel on the same cost level as competing foreign shipping companies.

Preferential treatment This involves measures which favour national flag vessels, such as cargo reservation schemes. The aim is to promote national flag shipping activities by providing a secure cargo base. Consequently foreign vessels are disadvantaged or excluded from participation. However, by inhibiting competition, inefficiency and inflexibility can be created, increasing costs and hampering technological development. In contrast it is argued that preferential treatment is necessary to promote a country's overall commercial and political interests.

Direct forms of cargo reservation include:

- National legislation, reserving part of the cargo in its foreign trade, for national flag vessels;
- Reduced customs duties for cargo transported in its national vessels.

Indirect forms are:

- Lower port dues and charges for national flag vessels;
- Priority for berthing and port handling for national flag vessels;
- Tax incentives for importers/exporters using the national flag;
- Restrictions in currency exchanges or unfavourable exchange rates for foreign shipowners;
- Favourable conditions, for the extension of import/export licences and letters of credit, to national flag vessels.

Other policies encourage or compel exporters to sell CIF of C & F, and importers to buy FOB (e.g. traditionally in East Europe and the ex Soviet Union and many developing countries). This system transfers vessel designation rights to the country concerned and allocates cargo to national flag vessels. Alternatively, a central booking office for imports/exports, can be established to allocate cargo to available tonnage and possibly direct cargo to national flag vessels.

Such policies can provoke retaliatory measures from other countries whose vessels are restricted or excluded from participating in a country's sea going foreign trade. Hence, if the policies are enforced over a long period, trade and relations with other countries could suffer. The implication is that a balance between national and international interests must be found.

In the context of this work we will need to consider to which maritime policy category the European Community (EC) belongs - in essence is it a free trade or protectionist organisation?

Examination of the nature of the EC's policies suggests that the answer we shall probably come to is most probably 'both'. On the one hand the EC talks of creating a single market which involves free trade within the Community: on the other, the EC acts to protect its members from the anti free market policies of the rest of the world.

Before we can examine the development and nature of EC shipping policies in any detail, it is necessary first to look into the background of the organisation.

The European Community

In 1946, after Europe had been devastated by World War II, Winston Churchill spoke in Switzerland of a 'United States of Europe'. However, when, after a series of negotiations, the original six members of the EC signed the Treaty of Rome in 1957, the UK declined to join. The original six were Italy, Belgium, Luxembourg, West Germany, France and the Netherlands. Little was done to strengthen this union until the 1970's recession encouraged the erection of barriers to trade in member states. Although protecting short term interests, in the long term Europe's ability to compete with the United States, Japan and newly industrialised countries was eroded. This led to pressure to find a common response to declining competitiveness (Hayer 1989).

The original six were joined in 1973 by UK, Denmark and Eire. In 1975 the UK voted in a referendum to stay in the EC. In 1981 Greece, 1986 Spain and Portugal, joined to make up the twelve present member states, extended geographically to incorporate the ex DDR in October 1990, as part of an expanded 'Germany'.

Up to 1992, Austria, Finland and Sweden have applied to become additional members of the EC. Hungary, Czechoslovakia and Poland also have talked about joining following recent changes in Eastern Europe, whilst Turkey, Norway, Malta, Cyprus and Switzerland are contemplating applications.

The Treaty of Rome

The European Economic Community (now commonly the European Community) was formed under the Treaty of Rome, signed on 25 March 1957. Its general aims included:

- drawing the people of Europe closer together;
- encouraging economic growth;
- improving living and working conditions.

As far as transport was concerned, the Treaty implied that the transport market must be organised in accordance with a market economy and that public intervention should occur only where it is otherwise impossible to proceed. The Community must ensure that restrictions to freedom to provide services are removed. At the same time the aim was to harmonise the overall framework in which modes and companies operate. Therefore the EEC was not to lose sight of the objective of optimising the transport process with a view to increasing competitiveness of the EEC, and improving service to the public.

In principle, the Treaty called for the creation of a market economy with minimal state intervention, limited restrictions on freedom to provide services, and no discrimination on the basis of nationality i.e. the principles of 'liberalization' and 'harmonization'.

The Community institutions

There are four main institutions in the Community:

- The Commission;
- The Council of Ministers;
- The European Parliament;
- The Court of Justice.

1) The Commission

The Commission, with its headquarters in Brussels, is the largest and most important institution of the European Community. It is the Commission's responsibility to implement the Treaty of Rome and the Single European Act (SEA) and to establish the genuinely free internal market. The Commission consists of twenty three directorate generals each responsible for a cultural or business area such as transport or fisheries. The Commission is also responsible for administration of the Community.

The main functions of the Commission include proposing community policy and legislation, which the Council then discuss and later adopt, amend or reject. Secondly, the Commission executes decisions taken by the Council of Ministers and supervises day to day management of community policies. Thirdly, the Commission acts as 'Guardian of the Treaties' and must initiate action against member states which do not comply with EC rules.

The Commission since 1986 has seventeen members appointed by member states, two from UK, France, Spain, Italy and Germany and one from each of the other countries.

2) The Council of Ministers

This is the decision making body, which adopts legislation on the basis of proposals from the Commission. Councils are attended by relevant ministers from member states and by commissioners who are present as of right and participate in discussions as an equal partner. The presidency is held by one member state representative who chairs council meetings. Presidency is rotated every six months. The council adopts the Commission's proposals by voting, either by unanimity, simple majority or qualified majority, depending on the points each member state holds and the issue under discussion. The nature of the proposal dictates the voting system used. In the context of this work, shipping decisions are always decided by the majority voting system.

3) The European Parliament

This is a directly elected body of 518 members, of which eighty one are from the UK. It has a wide range of responsibilities. Traditionally, its role has always been supervisory and consultative. It can scrutinize but not initiate legislation. It debates legislation passed by the council and can accept, reject of amend and pass the legislation by an absolute majority. If the European Parliament rejects legislation, it goes back to the council where it can only be passed with unanimity. Progress towards the SEM in 1993 has hastened the process of reforming the role of the EP and strengthened its decision making powers.

4) The Court of Justice

This court rules on implementation and application of community law. It has thirteen judges, including at least one from each country. Court judgements are binding in member states. (Hayer, 1989).

In addition to the four formal institutions directly involved in the community decision making process, the treaties created a number of other organisations which contribute to community life:

- The Economic and Social Committee for the EC has members representing producers, workers, farmers, consumers, self employed and trades unions, who have to be consulted by the council and commission on most of the legal provisions they propose adopting, though its opinions are in no way binding.
- The Court of Auditors, an innovation of 1977, verifies that all the rules are complied with as regards community revenue and expenditure.
- The European Investment Bank, set up to grant loans and give guarantees which facilitate the financing of projects in less developed regions, projects to

modernize/convert/develop activities and projects of interest to several member states which are on such a scale that individual member states cannot finance them entirely.

EC legislation and administrative procedure

EC legislation is enforced through four legal administrative procedures:

- Regulations - are generally binding and prevail over national law. They apply directly to all member states and need not be confirmed by member states parliaments.
- Directives - require member states to achieve a result by a certain date. A directive does not have legal force in member states but particular provisions may take direct effect if the directive is not duly implemented.
- Decisions - are specific and binding on those to who they are addressed. Financial obligations so imposed are enforceable in national courts.
- Recommendations and opinions - merely state the view of the community and suggest future policy and direction to member states.

The Single European Act (SEA)

Commitment to achieving a single market by the member states was reflected by the signing of the SEA (1987), which committed members to forming the single market by 31 December 1992. The single market was defined by the act as being, 'An area without frontiers, in which the free movement of goods, persons, services and capital is assured in accordance with the provisions of the Treaty of Rome'. (EC Commission 1989). The SEA came into force on 1 July 1987, and introduced changes to the Treaty of Rome such as the abandonment of unanimity required to pass EC legislation. The requirement became qualified majority interest except where vital national interests prevailed. Since then, more rapid progress has been made in achieving aims, and many original single market proposals have been approved by the council.

Through its institutional framework, and following the previously outlined procedures, the EC has been able to begin to implement a 'Common Transport Policy'. and it is the shipping section of this policy to which we will not turn our attention.

The shipping policy of the European Community

For many years, the EC did not have a shipping policy as the need for one was considered excluded by the Treaty of Rome: shipping was only mentioned in article 84, which enabled a shipping policy to be developed only if member states unanimously decided it was necessary.

Between 1957 and 1977 there was no shipping legislation. The first moves were made towards such agreements when the UK and Ireland joined the EC in 1973. These were both seafaring nations, and when the UK took the Council of Ministers to the European Court of Justice over a narrow seafaring issue and won, the need for a stated policy became evident. This need was increased by the wide recognition of the drastic decline of all EC registered fleets in the 1980's. (Commission for the European Communities 1989).

Between 1977 and 1985, several different shipping policy areas were developed; these can be summarised as follows:

a) Social issues: for example the free movement of people between countries; the harmonization of seafarers working conditions, and a range of social security measures.

In the 1980's, the Hollesen study outlined the different working conditions for seafarers in member countries which were based on varying national legislation. Although the council and parliament reviewed the study, and agreed that action was needed to integrate conditions, none was taken.

b) The right to establish shipping companies. The Treaty of Rome made it illegal for countries to show bias against any non national attempting to set up any form of company.

c) Competition within shipping was recognised early as a problem. It related especially to liner shipping conferences which violate the Treaty of Rome and a number of reports pinpointed the need for action as conferences are anti competitive. However, following strong economic and political arguments for their retention, no progress was made up to 1985 in reducing their role.

d) The Eastern Bloc has created problems for EC shipping. From 1977 onwards the Seefeld reports investigated this area. Eastern Bloc shipping has a conventional purpose of serving its own markets but also performs dubious defence exercises.

However, more significantly as most Eastern Bloc shipping companies were state owned, they did not need to operate commercially, only to earn hard convertible currency. Being able to charge less than cost because of state subsidy, these vessels were able to undercut western shipping. Although this was seen as unfair trading by the EC, little action could be taken. The EC did, however, set up a review of activities in the Eastern Bloc, with which it also entered into negotiations.

e) Safety and pollution legislation was agreed before 1985. The EC entered into negotiations with organisations such as BIMCO, and between 1978 and 1982, produced shipping related directives, for example, concerning pilots and tanker operations.

f) In 1979 the EC produced a regulation related to the UNCTAD code of conduct for liner shipping. The 'Brussels package' agreed by all member states, stated that ratification of the UNCTAD code by EC members was a requirement. When ratified, the 40/40/20 agreement was to apply to member states trade with developing countries, but not to trade between EC countries.

g) The Commission also recognised that the EC shipbuilding industry was facing economic difficulties and accepted that member states might have to provide subsidies. Although the EC was initially anti subsidy, a fixed percentage of ship cost (now eleven per cent) was allowed to be subsidised.

Overall, until 1985, there was little shipping policy to show for twenty eight years of the EC.

Stage 1 shipping policy

On 16 December 1986 the European Community Ministers of Transport agreed a maritime package which, combined with measures already adopted since 1977, forms the basis of a community policy in the maritime field.

As we have seen, in 1977, the European Community's adoption of a consultation procedure for shipping, and the 'Brussels package', provided for the accession of member states to the United Nations Code of Conduct for liner conferences. These measures were the outcome of a consensus among EC member states that a market oriented approach would be pursued for the organisation of world shipping.

In December 1984, the adoption of new policies made it possible to create a framework for EC shipping policy. Proposals annexed to the new policies were then discussed throughout the EC and members states and two years later, the council adopted a legislative package. This package included four regulations, which were outlined by Erdmenger and Stasinopoulos (1988), as follows:

Council Regulation (EEC) No. 4055/86. Freedom to provide services

This introduced the principle of freedom to provide services to intra community trade, distinguishing existing arrangements from future agreements. Applying to nationals and shipping companies of member states, it aims to prevent any member state from discriminating in favour of its own shipping companies to the disadvantage of shipping companies in another member state.

The regulation also applies to companies established outside the community if controlled by nationals of a member state and if their ships operate in accordance with the legislation of that member state.

This regulation also distinguishes between 'codist and non codist; trades: codist trades being those which are covered by the United Nations Code of Conduct. It calls for unilateral cargo restrictions by member states to be phased out by 1 January 1993. Other discriminatory cargo sharing arrangements between member states should be phased out or adjusted to comply with community legislation, with adaptation measures and any encountered problems reported to the Commission by 1 January 1993.

On non codist trades, where agreements are difficult to adjust properly, the council must take action if requested by a member state.

Future cargo sharing arrangements are permitted only when community cargo liner companies have no other means to ply for trade to and from third countries. If the council does not decide within six months on necessary action, a member state may initiate a cargo sharing agreement in compliance with community law. Finally, the council may extend the regulation to nationals of a third country who provide shipping services and are established in the community.

Council Regulation (EEC) No. 4013/86. Competition rules

This aims to apply treaty competition rules to shipping and affects all international shipping services to and from community ports, except tramp services. The aim is to balance the interests of conferences and shippers. It exempts liner cargo conferences from treaty provisions on restrictive practices, subject to conditions and obligations.

If an obligation is breached, the Commission may make a recommendation to the person concerned. If this is ignored the Commission may prohibit the person from carrying out that activity, or require performance of certain acts. Restrictive practices of third countries may prompt similar action, although council authorization is required to deal with conflicts in international law.

Council Regulation (EEC) No. 4057/86. Unfair pricing practices

This regulation, applying to liner trades, enables a compensatory duty to be imposed on non EEC shipowners, by the community, if the following conditions are cumulatively present:-

- There are 'unfair pricing practices' - defined as undercutting community shipping services, where this is made possible because the non EEC shipowners enjoy commercial advantages, such as subsidy.
- They cause injury.
- The interests of the community make intervention necessary.

The imposition of duties requires a council decision within two months of a proposal from the Commission.

Council Regulation (EEC) No. 4058/86. Coordinated action

This regulation covers bulk and liner cargoes, tramp services, passenger transport and movements between offshore installations. It deals with distortion of competition by governments giving preferential treatment to their own shipowners by flag discrimination.

It provides for coordinated community action where third countries restrict access of EEC shipping companies to ocean trades.

Coordinated action may be requested by member states from the Commission, which must make a proposal to the council within four weeks. The council may then decide on the application, extent and duration of counter measures. Member states unilaterally may undertake national measures if the council has not adopted a Commission proposal within two months. Such measures must be notified to the Commission and all member states.

A basic principle of the package is that a non protectionist policy is the best way to safeguard the application of commercial principles (required by the Treaty of Rome) in shipping.

It is also based on the assumption that it is in the interests of community shipping not to encourage a protectionist approach in the rest of the world. The community aims to continue a commercial regime by taking action against non commercial attacks upon it.

The community is monitoring the implications of the package. Some of the steps taken include:

17 May 1987 - Italy asked the Commission for approval of a draft shipping agreement between Italy and Algeria. The Commission proposed certain conditions, which the council modified in such a way that the Commission went to the European Court against the council decision.

18 November 1987 - the Commission started an investigation on alleged unfair pricing practices by Hyundai Merchant Marine of South Korea. Regulation 4057 was applied practically in this case in 1989, when it was reported that 'those that think the EC Commission is a slow, over bureaucratic, over legislative body, should think again. The Commission makes up the rules as it goes along, and can move at lightning speed.

Or so it would appear from the Sofrana Euro-Australia Line saga'. (Middleton, 1989b).

Briefly stated the sequence of events was this: on 4 January 1989, the EC Council of Ministers agreed to a Commission proposal to charge redressive duties on Hyundai Merchant Marine for 'unfair pricing' in the Europe/Australia trade. On 19 January, Hyundai announced the withdrawal of its service. On 20 january a new company, Sofrana Euro-Australia Lines GmbH announced it was taking over the service using the same ships, chartered from Hyundai and the same agency network. On 23 January the Commission's transport directorate DGVII notified member states that 'the evidence gathered so far allows the conclusion that the only difference between the Hyundai service and that of Sofrana is the name'. It urged the member states to carry on levying the duty on containers lifted in Europe by the service. Only on 26 January did the EC's DGVII (Transport) ask Sofeal for information about itself, and gave the company less than 24 hours to respond.

The main point to emerge from the case was that DGVII did not have to prove its contention about Sofeal; it simply stated it.

This case was important because:

- it demonstrated Commission procedures in a thorough investigation by the transport directorate;
- the judgement imposed a duty on the offending Korean line's tariff;
- evidence shows that the lesson of predatory pricing in EC trades has not been lost on some Eastern Bloc shipowners who have reformed without legal proceedings being necessary (Bott 1990).

Another recent case utilizing the 1986 package of regulations, began in 1987 when in July and September Maersk and OT Africa line filed complaints against four Europe-West Africa Conferences claiming that they were abusing their dominant position on the trade.

The EC has made a formal statement of objection to the conference carriers and could go on to impose penalties such as fines, or the withdrawal of the lines' bloc exemption from EC competition rules could be imposed (Anon 1. 1990).

The long running row over protectionism came to a head in the summer of 1989 when EC officials raided the offices of conferences to search for evidence of market manipulation. Since this time there has been a complete absence of any official word from the EC competition directorate, and the case remains unresolved, although during 1991 and into 1992 there are continuing rumours of EC developments which will affect the conference and consortia sector.

In implementing the package, the community has tried to ensure that competition is not distorted to provide conditions necessary to keep trades open to benefit transporters and shippers, and to discourage unfair pricing practices. Institutionally, the package was also important as it transferred significant power from the member states to the community.

Meanwhile, in March 1990, Eire took on the council presidency, and were keen to make further progress in applying the 1986 package of measures (Anon 2. 1990).

In June 1990 the Council of Transport Ministers met for two days in Luxembourg. The second day, chaired by Eire's Minister of Merchant Marine, was devoted to merchant shipping matters. On cabotage, ministers were still awaiting the opinion of the parliament and so were spared having to announce another failure to agree. (Anon 3. 1990).

Ministers welcomed the opportunity of examining the Commission document on the possibility of a group exemption from the competition rules for maritime and sea/land combined transport consortia and hoped an agreement could soon be reached. The Commission made a report on the extent to which the 1986 package of regulations had been applied. Finally, the council adopted two resolutions, one on preventing accidents causing marine pollution, the other on the safety of ferries.

Stage 2 shipping policy

Meanwhile no further progress had been made on developing stage 2 of the maritime policy until June 1989 when the EC attempted to deal with some of the more difficult issues.

Although no legislation has been produced by early 1992, procedures began on 3 August 1989 when the Commission's proposals, presented to the council on 5 June 1989, were published. The Commission's objectives were stated as being:

- to maintain an EC shipping fleet; and
- to maximise the number of European seafarers who could serve on that fleet.

It was recognised that the EC fleet could not be completely restored to previous levels or totally manned by EC nationals.

With these objectives in mind the Commission produced two separate documents, each of which will not be examined in some depth.

Paper 1: 'A future for the community shipping industry: measures to improve the operating conditions of community shipping' (Commission for the European Communities (1989))

The problems facing community shipping were identified as:

- The community lagged behind in modernization.
- The major decline of fleet size in the community had been caused in particular, by the cost of employing European Community seafarers.
- The decline of community fleets has an adverse influence on other factors; it damages the cost of transport to and from the community and affects employment, the balance of payments and defence.

The decline of the fleet was seen as a matter of concern for both the member states and the community. An assessment of the facts by the Commission lead to the conclusion that the downward trend in ownership, flag and crew of the community fleet, could only be stemmed by active policies. The challenge to the community was whether it should, and if so how, contribute to redressing the situation of the European shipping industry. The objectives of the community at stage 2 consisted of three elements; namely a commitment to community ownership, registration and crew to an extent dependent on the situation of the world shipping market; assessment of the structural changes taking place; and the extent to which member states and the community can assist the fleet. The overall broad aim was the reduction of disparities in operating conditions between the community fleets and their foreign competitors. The Commission believed that an 'action programme; was necessary to help the community shipping industry stem the decline of the fleet. This action programme had to meet a number of criteria:-

- it must be in line with the non protectionist shipping policy of the community, based on the principle of free and fair competition in world shipping;
- it must be effective in responding to the situation facing the industry;
- it must be capable of speedy introduction;
- it must prevent the growing divergence between member states policies which are tending towards a 'beggar they neighbour' effect and, as far as possible, reduce existing divergence;
- it must maintain, to the highest possible proportion, community employment in the sector and provide a perspective to those employed in it;
- it must not lead to the undermining of internationally agreed safety and environmental standards and employment conditions;
- it must not drive up freight rates to the detriment of shippers;
- it must be adapted to the financial possibilities of the member states.

Several policy initiatives were proposed in this first paper:

a) A community ship register: EUROS This was to be introduced on 1 January 1991, for vessels of less than 20 years, and greater than 520 grt. Run in parallel with national flags, EUROS would offer benefits such as:

- easier movement of ships between member states i.e. technical compatibility;
- mutual recognition of seafarer's qualifications;
- the 'opening-up' of cabotage to all vessels on the community register.

Vessels would be required to meet safety and certification levels of every member state; additionally, all officers plus half the crew had to be community nationals. Conditions of service for non community nationals had to meet ILO requirements (Commission of the European Communities 1989) - see Appendix 1 for further details of EUROS.

b) Manning and research The Commission suggested a research fund to decrease manning requirements on ships and hence lower costs.

c) Technical standardisation Presently, member states approve equipment separately and against national requirements which commonly leads to conflicts. Standardization, here, would aim to end such problems.

d) Social measures to improve working conditions For example, decreased hours, common training schemes, and mutual recognition of qualifications.

e) Environmental action This would ensure that the same standards of marine pollution prevention were applied in all ports.

f) Food aid exports EUROS flagged ships would receive priority to transport surplus foodstuffs as aid.

g) Definition of a shipowner A shipowner was defined as:

1a a national of a member state who has his domicile or usual residence in the member state;

1b a shipping company or firm which is formed in accordance with the law of a member state and which complies with the following requirements:

- the principal place of business must be situated and the effective control exercised in a member state; and
- the executive board must consist of persons the majority of whom are nationals of a member state or the majority of the shares must be owned by nationals of a member state having their domicile or usual residence in a member state.

2a a national of a member state who has his domicile or usual residence outside the community if his vessels are registered in that member state in accordance with its legislation;

2b a shipping company or firm established outside the community and controlled by nationals of a member state if its vessels are registered in that member state in accordance with its legislation.

This was an important issue to clarify as it affected cabotage rules.

h) Removal of restrictions on cabotage Because it attempts to open up the market, this has always been a politically contentious area. The Commission put forward the idea that all community countries should open their domestic shipping to EUROS vessels. Manning requirements would be the same as for the member state in question, which might conflict with EUROS requirements. It was also proposed that this item be reviewed in January 1993.

A 'get-out' clause was provided in that each member state could define specific routes which required subsidy to operate and were needed for public service reasons. Subject to Commission approval, these routes could then be reserved to national carriers.

In December 1990 European Community transport ministers agreed that a first phase of liberalizing cabotage shipping was to begin 'during 1993', amid strong opposition from the Greek and Italian Governments and some doubts over its legality.

The ministers agreed that the first phase should cover mainland cabotage and a second phase island cabotage. The legal doubts surrounded the setting of a date 'during 1993' - after the 1992 deadline - and the way that only 'mainland' shipping would be included in the first phase of the liberalization.

Greece is opposed to shipping cabotage because of the way it would hit lucrative island routes and there are said to be fears that it could lead to cuts in their fleet which they argue may be needed for defence reasons.

Northern European states, excluding France are generally in favour of liberalization and in the context of EC cabotage, the UK Secretary of State for Transport told his colleagues how the UK already allowed any foreign operator to compete with UK fleets on services out of British ports (Lloyds List 1990).

In February 1991, EC lawyers confirmed that the agreement reached in December was in breach of the Treaty of Rome (Lloyds List 1991a). The format of any subsequent agreement on cabotage, now forms part of Stage 3 shipping policy outlined in a later section.

Paper 2: Financial and fiscal measures concerning shipping operations with ships registered in the community (Commission for the European Communities (1989))

Whereas the first document set out proposals for legislation which could be drawn up, this second document was only advisory and mainly concerned subsidy.

The Commission recognised that much community shipping was already heavily subsidized, and that this was grossly distorting the market. However, the Commission agreed to approve subsidies to shipping operations under some circumstances, and within a number of constraints.

Subsidy sometimes appeared to be in the common interest because it could help to retain community ships, under community flags, and help to employ community seamen. It was, however, decided that any state aid should not exceed a ceiling defined by the lowest relevant cost difference. This would be the gap between the lowest operating costs within the community, and those of a typically flagged out vessel. Also, subsidy had to be transparent - with all details made public; time limited; and should not contribute to increasing or maintaining capacity in sectors where there was already a surplus.

Finally, only three types of subsidy were to be allowed, i.e.:

- those involving social security payments,
- those for training, and
- differential tax regimes.

Each country had to submit subsidy plans and have them approved by the Commission before they could be implemented.

The Stage 2 package was only a set of proposals which it was hoped would be implemented by 1993. In practice, by February 1992, no relevant legislation had been passed with both 'free market' advocates (UK, Eire, Denmark), and protectionists (Greece, Spain, Italy, France), rejecting the proposed policies. Whatever other components of the single market will be in place by the end of 1992, it is likely that a common European shipping policy will be present only in skeletal form. (Lloyds Shipping Economist, 1990). Nearly five years have passed since the European Commission's first attempt to shape a common shipping policy, but fundamental differences remain between EC members.

The latest and final moves so far can be found in an internal EC paper outlining a new EC maritime policy, drawn up by Dr Bangemann, Vice President of the European Commission. According to Dr Bangemann the advent of the single market within the EC will double the present volumes of cross border transport - the vase majority of it by sea - by the year 2000. At the same time international trade, ninety per cent carried by shipping, is expected to continue growing (Lloyds List 29 August 1991).

To prepare the EC for the upturn Bangemann is advocating a European maritime agency, primarily as a forum for promoting cooperation between all parts of the industry and EC governments. He dismissed previous maritime policy as 'out of date' (Lloyds List 30 August 1991).

In an interview with Lloyds List on 3 September 1991, Dr Kroeger, Managing Director of the Association of German Shipowners, stated that the test for an effective European maritime policy is 'whether it offers conditions which would make the industry want to stay in Europe'. Although commenting that Bangemann's proposals were welcome he felt that they had not gone beyond a 'very initial phase'.

On 28 September 1991 it was reported in the Telegraph that the European Commission had set up a forum to examine community maritime policies and to find ways of making EC shipping, shipbuilding and maritime services more competitive. The forum was asked to produce a report and recommendations by summer 1992 (Telegraph 28 September 1991).

While there is broad agreement that the community ought to have a modern and efficient merchant fleet, and that it should not be dependent on protectionist or bilateral policies, the reduction of these general principles into detailed and practical measures has so far proved extremely difficult.

It is likely that the main issues of aid, cabotage and EUROS will remain unresolved for a long time yet. The largest objection to cabotage comes from Italy who with a domestic market of twenty million passengers and sixty million tonnes of freight has, perhaps, the most to lose; although objections on this front have come also from Greece, Spain, Portugal and France.

Progress may be made on less controversial issues such as training and certification, marine safety and interchangeability of qualifications. But little of this will address the competitive position of European shipping and consequently owners will probably continue to seek their own solutions such as flagging out to reduce costs. Moreover, as John Steele of UK based Prisma Transport Consultants recently suggested, there is a risk that if the decline of the EC fleet continues there will be a tendency towards protectionism. This, he says, could provoke similar protectionism throughout the world. Alternatively, failure to provide positive policies for Europe's shipowners could provoke a hardening of attitudes against cheap shipping and bring flags of convenience into the firing line. (Anon 4. 1990).

The creation of a single market by 1 January 1993, as outlined earlier, relies upon the removal of present market barriers, and the passing of much legislation, including that relating to but separate from Stage 2. Shipping legislation is already behind the necessary rate of action.

There are three types of broad barrier to the creation of a single market; attempts to remove these have affected shipping as follows:

1   Physical barriers including border checks and customs points. Attempts to remove these in shipping have included:
    i)   the introduction of the single administrative document to ease movement of goods;
    ii)   a common integrated customs tariffs for goods moving within or into the EC;
    iii) a number of smaller proposals, e.g. the appraisal of consistent VAT rates and abolition of customs checks.

2   Technical barriers relating to technicalities of vessels, taxation and legal frameworks. These are being removed in three ways:
    i)   since 1983 the Commission has been able to override any national technical legislation acting as a barrier to trade;
    ii)   attempts have been made to regulate banking and insurance industries;
    iii) work is being carried out to produce mutually recognised standards of qualification.

3   Fiscal barriers relate to monetary rates and excise duties of moving goods internationally. Attempts to remove these barriers have included those relating to public procurement. It is estimated that fifteen per cent of EC GNP is spent by governments. The EC would like to see open tendering, so that the government of any member state could be supplied by nationals of any other member state, and would be required to assess tenders from all other states.

Although some progress has been made towards the creation of a truly single market, shipping is one of the specific areas in which the EC is well behind schedule.

Looking at the European scene, an article in Lloyds Shipping Economist, February 1990, highlighted that 'it is likely that the main issues will remain unresolved for a long time yet, possibly beyond 1992'. (Anon 1990).

Universal agreement on policy is obviously difficult because of the wide range of views and the varying interests of different countries. Despite the need for a common EC policy on shipping, very different regimes presently exist within member states providing one of the main reasons for the development of a coherent community policy.

The remainder of this paper will look at the position of the UK in terms of state shipping policy, and its contrasts with that of the community as a whole. The UK has been a maritime nation throughout its history and, as an island nation, has a very heavy dependence on foreign trade. Until recently the UK Government operated subsidies (operating, construction, loans); tax benefits and customs rebates; credit facilities for export orders, and also had one of the largest public ownerships and substantial shareholdings. This, however, is very different to the situation today, as we shall see in the next section which looks at UK shipping policy in some detail.

United Kingdom shipping policy

The aim of this section is to examine the contrast between EC policy towards shipping and that of one member state - the UK. Before studying UK shipping policy in any detail, it is necessary to consider the need, if any, for such a policy. It is helpful here to compare some past and present statistics.

In 1950, Britain had the biggest merchant fleet in the world with twenty one per cent of all tonnage; by 1990 it was the eleventh biggest with two per cent. There are 3.8 million deadweight tons under mainland British registration, compared with a peak of 52 million in 1975 (Telegraph 1991). The fleet's average age is exceeded only by those of Panama and Liberia. At least as significant, there are now fewer than 18,000 British seafarers against 58,000 in 1976, and there has been precious little training in the past 30 years. (The Independent 1990). Table 1 gives an indication of the extent of the decline of the UK fleet in relation to other EC countries, up to 1988 (Commission of the European Communities 1989), and suggests that its decline is the most severe of all EC member state fleets.

The British fleet faces two threats; it desperately needs renewing, but few owners can afford to order new ships; and those ships that are built, are unlikely as things stand, to be placed on the UK registry or to be manned by a British crew. Already, most Ensigns are on the sterns of Hong Kong or Isle of Man vessels.

In analyzing the UK fleet's decline three questions need to be asked. First does the decline of the fleet matter in itself? Second, is there a link between the size of the merchant fleet and London's continuing success as a service centre? And third if the answer to either of these is yes, what can be done about it?

The need for a UK shipping policy

If the financial returns on investments in ships are insufficient, there is no sound commercial reason for UK companies to invest in ships, let alone keep them under the UK flag and man them with UK seafarers. Logically, UK commercial shipping

Table 1

Merchant fleets[a] - Analysis by community ship registers[b]

FLAG	1975		1980		1984		1985		1986		1987		1988	
	No of ships	MGRT	No of ships	MGRT	No of ships	MGRT	No of ships	MGRT	No of ships	MGRT	No of ships	MGRT	No of ships	MGRT
B	99	1.3	105	1.7	125	2.3	124	2.3	117	2.3	112	2.1	103	1.9
DK	950	4.3	746	5.2	643	5.1	607	4.8	575	4.5	588	4.6	549	4.2
FR	562	10.4	465	11.6	405	8.6	381	7.9	415	5.6	315	4.1	291	4.2
FRG	1,578	8.2	1,492	8.0	1,424	6.0	1,447	5.9	1,410	5.3	1,099	4.1	923	3.7
GR	2,561	22.4	3,634	39.4	2,673	34.9	2,353	30.9	1,995	28.3	1,679	23.4	1,584	21.8
IRL	51	0.2	63	0.2	69	0.2	67	0.2	69	0.1	64	0.1	66	0.1
IT	1,222	9.9	1,154	10.9	978	9.0	956	8.6	947	7.6	943	7.6	930	7.4
NL	802	5.4	690	5.3	635	4.0	630	3.7	644	3.8	620	3.4	565	3.2
PORT	169	1.1	121	1.2	109	1.4	112	1.3	100	1.0	77	0.9	76	0.9
SP	804	4.8	817	7.5	765	6.4	740	5.6	674	4.9	609	4.4	554	3.8
UK	2,246	32.2	1,931	26.1	1,216	14.9	1,135	13.3	1,026	10.6	916	7.51	871	7.2
EEC 11	11,044	100.2	11,218	117.1	9,042	92.8	8,552	84.5	7,972	74.0	7,022	63.2	6,512	58.5

a) Merchant fleet excluding fishing vessels, tugs, dredgers, ice breakers, research vessels, supply ships, tenders and miscellaneous. Vessels 100 GRT and over.

b) These figures include various 'second' registers e.g. the Isle of Man and Kerguelen Islands.

Source: Lloyds Register of Shipping, Statistical Tables

companies cannot be expected to provide manpower and expertise for the wider maritime infrastructure. (Moreby and Springett 1989). Many companies may conclude that owning ships is neither essential nor compatible with their commercial prosperity. However, some organisations believe that ship owning is vital to the national interest because of:

National needs

a) National/economic reasons for UK citizens to remain involved in the manning, technical operation and trading of ships are:

- to provide expertise for the wider marine related activities in the country;
- to have the capability of exploiting new trading opportunities and resources from the sea.

b) Preserving a UK fleet will prevent a drain on the balance of payments. To maintain a surplus in the sea transport account, UK owned ships must carry forty per cent of exports, and importer payments should be no greater than forty five per cent of revenue received from abroad by the UK. This would also involve carrying a third of the country's imports and require an increase in the UK fleet size. The fleet now carries less than a quarter of its own trade (Moreby and Springett 1989).

c) There are social and political reasons for maintaining a UK flag fleet. Britain's merchant navy has a vital role to play in any period of tension or war, as regards carriage of troops and equipment, defence and replenishment of the country during hostilities. Other reasons include the maintenance of British presence in major trading nations ports, and protection of the environment. British ship owners are under UK Government control and are responsive to needs of British importers/exporters. Their very existence provides competition necessary to ensure that foreign shipping interests are also responsible to British needs. If British controlled ships ceased to exist the country would lose control over its vital lifeline. (GCBS 1987).

Maintaining a UK flag fleet will also preserve influence on European and international bodies affecting shipping and trade. The UK's influence will fall in relation to all marine international organisations - for example IMO, the Baltic and International Maritime Council and the International Chamber of Shipping - if there is a further decline of people of standing with maritime expertise.

Manpower shortages

A shortage of officers was first predicted for 1990. Actual levels of officer cadet intakes in recent years made it impossible to avoid these and future shortfalls; and as 1989 entrants will not qualify before 1993, the fleet manpower base can only be stabilized from 1992 onwards (Moreby and Springett 1989).

The maritime infrastructure

a) Maritime infrastructure and component activities of the UK shipping industry fall into three categories:

- Supportive activities - city based and commercially related.

- Dependent activities - located regionally and related to ports, cargo and marine technology.
- Interdependent - located regionally and commercial or technical in nature.

According to Moreby and Springett (1989), of the 83,692 people involved in this maritime infrastructure in the UK, 10,915 require essential seafaring experience and 20,997 essential shipping experience. Their total annual wages could be as much as £1,298 million, the value added in tax then being at least £325 million.

Each of the activities also requires expertise in other maritime fields outside their own organisation and available for consultation in the locality.

Commercial freedom

a) Maintaining a national fleet could help to keep shipping and offshore markets free and commercial and avoid exploitation by potential shipping oligopolies avoid overseas government intervention and protectionism, and distortions in liner freight and offshore service rates.
b) Presence of a significant UK fleet can influence the safe carriage of passengers and crew, and maintain standards of service and quality with respect ot pollution avoidance, and improvement of safety at sea.
c) Maritime activities have a large contribution to make to the UK economy, the highest ranking of these are as follows:

- offshore oil and gas;
- the city e.g. insurance and finance;
- owning/operating/managing ships.

Growth

It is argued that the UK national fleet must be kept large enough to maintain the ability to exploit new commercial opportunities.

Critical levels

The study by Moreby and Springett in July 1989 showed clearly that, on three criteria - its ability to meet the country's defence requirements; its ability to contribute positively to the balance of payments; and, its ability to man the projected UK fleet with UK people - the privately financed UK owned/registered fleet has now fallen below its critical level and could be threatened with extinction.

Scarrot (1989) expressed similar views on the importance of maintaining a national fleet. On the defence front, a UK Government arrangement with flag of convenience states allowing for recall of UK ships in times of emergency, was referred to by Scarrot as ' a cap-in-hand approach to crisis', which required voluntary cooperation from shipowners. He was also concerned at falling national manpower levels, and highlighted the fact that in recent defence exercises, only one of thirty four ships was British.

Mounting fears over such deficiencies have prompted the government to launch a merchant navy reserve so that officers no longer at sea might be recalled in an emergency. Already dubbed 'Dad's Navy', it only offers a short term solution due to the age of many of its officers.

Comparison with other UK industries

The UK Chamber of Shipping has stated clearly its belief that shipowning is vital to the national interest. As well as emphasizing the concerns previously mentioned, it also pointed to the fact that the UK shipping industry is almost alone among British industries in its full exposure to foreign, and often unfair competition. For example, UK manufacturing industry operates behind the external tariff policies of the EC, UK agriculture is supported by the Common Agricultural Policy and civil aviation is defended by government agreements.

Long term future of the City of London as a maritime centre

Lord Sterling of Plaistow, Chairman of P & O, and ex president of the Chamber of Shipping, believes that the long term future of London as a centre of shipping is intimately linked to the size of the British merchant fleet. 'The strength of the maritime associated industries is strongly dependent on people who have worked on ships and who have come ashore' he says. 'Thousands of people working in the city started off at sea'. He believes that unless the decline in the merchant marine is stopped, youngsters will not contemplate a marine career, and the shrinkage will thus become self reinforcing (The Independent 1990).

It would appear that there is a strong need for an identifiable UK shipping policy. We now need to consider the action taken by the UK Government to date, and the possibilities for further action.

What the UK Government has done to help since 1979

The Chamber of Shipping readily acknowledges that the UK Conservative Governments since 1979 have taken action of benefit to shipping. Political action against the tide of protectionism and agreements negotiated within the European Community have been helpful. So has the government's Merchant Shipping Act of 1988 which made provision for the implementation of measures to provide financial assistance with the training of seafarers and with repatriation costs.

The intention of the scheme to provide financial assistance with the repatriation of crews was to 'reimburse shipping companies for a substantial proportion of crew transfers of seafarers ordinarily resident in the the British Isles and serving on ships registered in the UK, Isle of Man or Channel Islands where the crew changes take place outside the United European trading area of Bergen to Cadiz...' (Standing Committee B 1988). A sum of about £5 million was to be provided.

The Transport Committee in 1988, welcomed the assistance which was intended to 'reduce the differential between the cost of employing UK and third world crews', and hoped for success in meeting the objective of helping to stem the decline in the number of British seafarers employed on UK ships.

On the training front, the Government has taken powers under the Act to provide assistance with training costs by helping offset the salary costs of cadets currently met by shipping companies (Government Publication 1988).

It also hoped to enable the industry to take greater advantage of existing provision of the funding of education and training. The government, therefore, was providing special assistance of £3.5 million p.a. with the aim of substantially increasing cadet numbers.

The UK Parliamentary Under Secretary of State for Transport stated in 1990 that he hoped that 'within a short period of time we would see at least a doubling in the number of officer cadets going for training'.

However, the government had already dealt a blow to investment in shipping in the 1984 budget, when it withdrew the previous tax allowances for investment in shipping. The lower rate of corporation tax, the universal twenty five per cent writing down allowances and their subsequent extension to second hand ships and the extension of the business expansion scheme to investment in ships, have not, according to the Chamber of Shipping compensated adequately for the damage done in 1984.

In response to the question 'is the government going to leave the UK shipping industry to the mercy of international market forces?', Lord Brabason of Tara, as Minister for Shipping replied in 1990

> No, we need to look at the complete picture. On one side there are the capital allowances, but on the other hand we have one of the lowest rates of corporation tax in the developed countries. And we certainly have one of the lowest rates of income tax in the EC, and more generally in the developed countries. They (the shipowners) have done quite well, in common with the rest of UK industry'. (Bray & Gaskell 1989).

As for direct help to the industry, Lord Brabazon cited the 1988 Merchant Shipping Act which, as we have seen, was generally focused on training and repatriation matters. He pointed to the £3.5 million in training funds, the £5 million raised BES (state aid) limit, and the relaxation of tax exemption rules for seafarers. 'Altogether the package could be worth up to £25 million - and that's new money'.

In response to the argument that London will not maintain its position as a shipping and insurance centre if not enough people are entering the service, Lord Brabazon said 'the decline over the past 10 years has had apparently no effect on London, so I cannot follow the logic of the argument'.

John Lusted of the Chamber of Shipping admitted that 'the government are doing something', but continued 'they are helping around the fringes. We need more, especially for training'. (Bray & Gaskell 1989).

The GCBS commenting in 1989, believed that there were a wide range of further measures which the British Government could take to promote the British shipping industry; and that overall, action was needed on three fronts:

a) To tilt the balance in favour of reinvestment in ships rather than other industries of lesser national importance but higher rate of return.

b) To bridge the gap between the cost of running a ship with a British crew compared to a foreign crew.

c) To improve British ships trading prospects and reduce other, government imposed, operation costs.

The GCBS estimates that £1 billion of revenue deferred over five years through the reintroduction of some tax benefits would generate £7.5 billion of foreign exchange earnings over fifteen years. The Treasury has ignored this argument since 1984 and it appears that it is unlikely to be convinced otherwise.

More specifically, the GCBS put forward the following measures.

a) Measures to aid reinvestment

i)   Roll over relief for balancing charges: i.e. for the Treasure to forego tax repayments on the excess of sale value over written down value of ships providing receipts were reinvested in another ship within three years of disposal of the old one. This would enable renewal and updating of the fleet whilst mirroring practices in Spain, Netherlands and Germany. The benefit was estimated at £12 million for every 100 ships.

ii)   A fifty per cent ship allowance as an incentive for investment in ships.

b) Measures to assist running costs

i)   Income tax and social security charges: The GCBS suggested that contributions to National Insurance by the employer should be reduced by a further fifty per cent; whilst income tax on seafarers earnings should be eliminated. The latter would remove two thirds of the cost advantage of Isle of Man and similar registries.

ii)   A merchant navy strategic reserve contract, could be entered into for each UK owned ship kept on a UK or designated register in recognition of its availability to the UK Government in times of emergency. The payment would need to be set at about £150,000 p.a. per ship of full UK crew, in order to yield the difference between Isle of Man and cheapest crewing.

iii)   A crew related allowance, payable in respect of each British seafarer employed by UK owners on their ships, irrespective of flag. A merchant navy reserve allowance would ensure the continued seagoing employment of active mariners.

c) Measures to improve trading prospects and reduce costs

i)   Delegation of surveys to classification societies. The GCBS continues to urge the Department of Transport to accept hull and machinery surveys carried out by the major classification societies.

ii)   Reform of the Merchant Shipping Act. At present this permits the seafarers unions to evade the requirement of the Trade Union Act 1984 to hold a ballot before calling their members out on strike. It would place shipowners in the same position as other employers if this section of the Act were repealed.

d) Action within the EC

Further measures promoted by the government could provide benefits to shipping. Positive measures would be:

i)   To allow the unimpeded transfer of ships that meet internationally accepted standards onto the British register if they have previously been acceptable to any other EC administration.

ii)   To accept, for all shipboard positions any EC national with an appropriate certificate of competency issued by another member state.

iii)   Action to implement the Lome Convention which calls for free shipping relations between the EC and the Lome States. These are flaunted by many Lome States who nevertheless enjoy the benefits of the convention.

iv) Elimination of cabotage restrictions of many other EC states. British ships are presently excluded from coastal trades of some community partners whilst any ship can trade around the British coasts.

v) Negotiation of Stage II of the EC shipping policy intended to improve competitive positions of EC shipowners with respect to non EC competitors, and which also covers many of the cabotage and vessel transfer issues noted above.

Equally, defensive action is needed:

i) To challenge the intention of the Commission to remove the VAT exemption for passenger fares, within and between EC countries, and to ensure the proposed imposition of VAT on all expenditure needed to operate a passenger or cargo ship will not increase operating costs of companies by net VAT payments or excessive administration costs.

ii) To retain duty free sales until the last moment when the harmonization of EC taxes and duties is achieved. These sales effectively subsidize passenger and freight traffic and, if lost, would necessitate increases in fares and tariffs to the order of twenty five per cent to maintain present quality of service.

e) Channel Tunnel

Action is needed to ensure ferry companies can compete with the tunnel. The tunnel will provide such competition as to render irrelevant current UK Government restrictions on the ferry companies' ability to rationalize services. Operators must be allowed to co operate, as do liner companies within conferences, as long as they meet requirements of the EC competition regulation. This provides adequate consumer protection.

In 1988 the UK Parliamentary Transport Committee's first report on 'Decline in the UK - Registered Merchant Fleet' (Transport Committee 1988) established that 'the UK needs a merchant fleet' but identified the difficulty in convincing the government that it should give tangible recognition to that fact.

In the hope of ensuring the continued existence of the fleet, the committee then made a series of recommendations; the most important of which were as follows:

a) That the Department of Transport institute random checks of surveys carried out and that, if the surveys carried out by any particular classification society are shown to be seriously inadequate, the department ensure that no further surveys are delegated to that society.

b) That urgent and sympathetic consideration be given to the proposals for roll over relief for balancing charges: if ships were not purchased there would be no cost to the Treasury from roll over relief; if they were, this would help the efficiency and competitiveness of the UK shipping industry.

c) That the business expansion scheme (ie state aid) limit of £5 million be raised substantially bearing in mind the high capital costs of ships.

d) That the government does not hesitate to use the power it has taken to introduce a test of establishment of operators who wish to carry out cabotage in UK coastal waters if the discussions in the EC on the abolition of cabotage are not brought to a satisfactory conclusion within a reasonable period of time.

e) That the government should look again at the whole question of employers' national insurance contributions in respect of foreign going seafarers. The combined employer/employee contributions to National Insurance are about thirteen per cent of the wage bill. A reduction on the grounds that foreign going seafarers will inevitably use the facilities of the National Health Service less than people permanently resident in the country would be a help to the industry.

f) That the present practice with regard to deduction of tax from seafarers employed by ship management companies should continue.

g) That urgent consideration be given to amending the statutory regulations which prevent Inland Revenue from deducting tax from an employee where an employer should have operated PAYE.

h) That the sum made available by government for seafarer training be doubled.

i) That the government encourage a campaign in which all interested bodies should be invited to participate with the clear aim of improving the image and stressing the opportunities of the UK shipping industry.

j) That the arrangements for repatriating UK owned vessels registered in foreign countries be concluded as a matter of the highest priority.

k) That, if the Merchant Navy Reserve is not effective, the government give consideration to further measures.

l) That periodic training of the reserve be introduced.

There are signs that more and more governments see shipping as too important to be left to market forces: approximately seventy nations give aid to their fleets. The formation of a British merchant navy reserve signifies that shipping is more than just another business but, despite repeated pleas from shipowners and an all party committee of MPs, the Parliamentary Maritime Group - the UK Government has done nothing to help avoid a crisis. In the works of Scarrot 'rigid free market Government policies continue to sink what little now remains of the UK owned and registered fleet' (Scarrot 1989).

More recently in 1991, the change of British prime minister and the consequential changes which ensued, encouraged further pressure from the British shipping industry. As the new Chancellor of the Exchequer settled in at Number 11 Downing Street, NUMAST, the UK ship officers trades union, sent him a report outlining the action needed to enable British shipping to prosper in the 1990's. (Telegraph 1991). The report - which sought help in the 1991 Budget - warned that fiscal measures were urgently needed to help British shipping compete on equal footing in world màrkets. (NUMAST 1991).

Despite these pressures, the Chancellor's budge on 19 March 1991 failed to announce measures to prevent widespread flagging out of what remains of the UK fleet.

Norman Lamont offered no concessions on the two main measures sought by the GCBS - a 100 per cent ship allowance and waiving of the income tax and national insurance costs of UK seafarers (GCBS 1990). Instead he chose to double the amount of time UK seafarers are allowed to spend in the country without paying UK tax from 90 to 183 days, as a measure designed to ensure that there is a sufficient pool of UK seafarers available to meet defence needs during time of war.

Lord Sterling as the then president of the GCBS said 'I find it extraordinary that the government, recognising the strategic requirement as unanimously agreed by the government - industry working party, has not been prepared to introduce measures vital to rebuild the UK flag fleet manned by British seafarers'. (Lloyds List 1991c).

As we have seen, the 1991 UK Budget Statement in March, provided little help to the ailing UK merchant shipping industry. Despite this, or perhaps because of it, the UK industry, and the GCBS in particular, have continued to campaign on behalf of the fleet.

As yet, there has been little tangible success, and the prospect of a General Election in 1992, has done little to advance prospects of progress.

In May 1991, Malcolm Rifkind, the relatively new Secretary of state for Transport in the UK, who includes within his brief the UK shipping industry, in an interview with Lloyds List (1991d) gave an indication of his priorities for this sector. Although expressing considerable sympathy for the industry, this did not extend as far as providing direct help. His views conformed closely to those of Thatcherism of the 1980's. To quote him :

> We are sympathetic to the concerns expressed by British shipping. But the Conservative Government tries to help industry as a whole by a series of measures to reduce the overall tax burden. It would be very unusual to make an exception and we would then receive similar requests from other industries.

He made it clear that it was for the Ministry of Defence to assess the defence impact of the decline of the fleet, whilst in terms of trade, the British flag had no particular role to play. In fact, 'flagging out was not something peculiar to the UK'. Commercial forces had to dictate flag choice, and flag of vessel had no effect on the visible trade balance of payments.

In late May 1991, Rifkind produced a new policy initiative for transport, including the shipping sector, but his comments were limited and largely dismissed by the industry as inadequate. To quote Lloyds List of 30 May 1991 :

> Maritime hearts beat a little faster when Mr Rifkind said that he proposed to say something briefly about aviation and shipping. Brief was the operative description with a single short paragraph suggesting that the government needed to explore new opportunities that may exist for enhanced coastal shipping and for greater use for freight of our many canals.

No words on international shipping, nor on the state of the UK merchant fleet. Meanwhile, the decline continued.

The debate, albeit rather one sided and dominated by industry statements rather than substantial ones from the government, continued through June 1991. A report in Tradewinds, the International Shipping Gazette, suggested that the government and shipowners in the UK were facing severe embarrassment because they had run out of UK flagged vessels to use for training under the £3.5 million per annum scheme introduced under the 1988 Merchant Shipping Act. Foreign flagged vessels would now have to be used and the rules of the scheme had had to be widened to allow this. Although this was predicted to have little impact on the quality of training, it was a political embarrassment, increasing pressure on the government to do something about the fleet's decline. To quote John Newman, General Secretary of the UK Officers' Union, NUMAST :

> This highlights the total illogicality of the Government's approach to shipping. The Government gives a teaspoon of aid for training and then ignores the needs of the fleet in general by refusing aid in the budget.

The aim of the scheme, according to the government itself, was to stem the decline in UK merchant seamen, and it has been successful in raising trainees from 147 in 1988 to 535 in 1990, but the original design of the scheme allowed for training only on UK flagged vessels. This has had to be relaxed.

Further bad news followed on 20 June (Lloyds List, 1991e) when the Shell Oil

Company announced that it was planning to cut its tanker fleet by nearly a half, from ninety to fifty vessels, resulting in a major loss of UK merchant seamen jobs.

In July, two further major events occurred. Under government procedures in the UK, the budget proposals of March do not become effective until the Finance Bill gains parliamentary approval and Royal Assent in July of each year. In the Telegraph (July 1991), it was noted that hopes had been raised that a rebellion by backbench Conservative MPs might produce the measures sought by NUMAST and the GCBS, to revive UK shipping, which had not been included in the March budget statement. More than 170 MPs, including a hundred Conservatives, had supported formally, two amendments calling for tax incentives to boost the UK shipping industry - including tax allowances for investment in new ships; and tax and national insurance exemptions for UK seafarers. The minor tax incentives for seafarers announced in the March budget had already been agreed in the Finance Bill.

However, by late July efforts to amend the Finance Bill were ended by the Speaker of the House of Commons, who refused to allow a debate on the issue on procedural grounds, accusing pro shipping MPs of 'over lobbying' and hence, breaking an unwritten parliamentary rule. The reaction of the UK shipping industry was contradictory. On the one hand, it was appalled by the lack of progress; on the other it welcomed the substantial press reports that followed, emphasizing the plight of the UK fleet.

The second event was the publication in July by the UK marine officers' trades union NUMAST, of a report on the UK fleet and defence. This report, aimed at the UK Government, outlined the need for a substantial merchant marine for defence reasons. It commented on the decline of the fleet, and noted a UK Department of Transport report on shipping and defence that had been published earlier that year.

In that report, the Department of Transport had concluded that :

- Parent ownership rather than country of registry was a 'close proxy' for ultimate control of a vessel.

NUMAST disputed this, as few vessels were flagged even under Crown Dependencies whereby vessels could be requisitioned by the government.

- There would be no fleet decline between 1990 and 1995.

By mid 1991 a decline had already manifested itself. NUMAST also commented that no account had been taken of fleet age, location, type or condition.

The NUMAST report went on to point out that the Merchant Navy Reserve had attracted only eight per cent of its required numbers; that only eight out of 142 ships chartered for the Gulf War were UK flagged; that ship shortages did exist in the Gulf War and that delays to the allied forces had been reported as a result; that the cost of requisitioning foreign ships had been up to three times the market rate; that a number of foreign seafarers had refused to sail to the Gulf; and that the US response to such problems had been to inject $1 billion into their own merchant marine. So far the NUMAST report has produced no action from the government, but clearly the fight for the UK fleet continues.

Conclusions

The main objectives of this paper were to :

1   Assess the UK maritime industry's view of the shipping policies of the UK and the EC.
2   Obtain an assessment of the relative success or failure in policy formulation of each with respect to shipping.
3   Identify the problems that any conflict between the UK and the EC policies may present.
4   Suggest ways forward for the future.

From the research it has emerged that a government stimulated shipping policy is important to provide direction to an economically and strategically vital industry. European Community shipping policy is very slowly emerging based upon the free trade ideal, and is consequently anti subsidy, anti protectionist and pro competition. It also became apparent that the UK similarly favoured a free market approach but in contrast to the EC, deliberately did not have a coherent policy for shipping, arguing that a laissez faire approach achieved the same ends without the drawback of state interference in the market.

Discussions with the UK shipping industry revealed that in their opinion neither the UK or the EC had a clear shipping policy; and that those policies which were evident appeared to be mismatched, placing UK companies at a disadvantage with respect to other EC members. Companies emphasized that the lack of any recognisable policies meant that they had no guidance, also that throughout the community, there was a need to 'level the playing fields'.

This research has revealed a strange paradox. It is notable that both the EC and the UK believe in free trade, and favour the 'laissez faire' approach; however, the EC is pushing this ideal through the slow formation of a directed policy, whereas the UK appears to have no intentions under current or future administrations, of forming a maritime policy of any note.

As far as the future is concerned, it is inevitable that the EC will continue to push for 'harmonization and liberalization; and that we will eventually see Stage 3 of a Community Shipping Policy emerging. This may result in a slowing down of the decline of the EC fleet. Conversely, the decline of the UK fleet looks likely to continue. Despite a change in Prime Minister during 1990 and continual industrial pressure, little progress has been made towards a clear UK shipping policy and this situation appears unlikely to change in the foreseeable future. Consequently, the paradoxical situation at present, and the conflict between the European Community and the United Kingdom look set to continue for the foreseeable future.

References

Anon 1 (1990), 'Lines face penalties' Freight News Express, 2 July.
Anon 2 (1990), 'Brussels report', Transport, 11, 3.
Anon 3 (1990), 'Brussels report' Transport, 11, 6.
Anon 4 (1990), 'EC and 1992, Lloyds Shipping Economist, 12, 1.
Arbuthnott, H. and Edwards, G. (1979), Common Man's Guide to the Common Market, Macmillan Press Ltd.
Bott, A. (1990), 'Playing Field Imbalances', Transport, 11, 7.
Bray, J. (1988), 'EEC legal regime', Seatrade Business Review, March/April, pp. 19-21.

Bray, J. and Gaskell, P. (1989), 'No Policy : No Strategy : No guiding Star', Seatrade Business Review, March/April.

Bredimas, A.E. (1981), 'The Common Shipping Policy of the EEC', Common Market Law Review, pp. 9-32.

Commission for the European Communities (1979), The Community Today

Commission for the European Communities (1985), 'Progress towards a common transport policy', 19 March.

Commission for the European Communities (1989), 'A future for the Community Shipping Industry: Measures to improve the operating conditions of community shipping' COM (89) 266 FINAL, 3 August

Commission for the European Communities (1989), 'Financial and fiscal measures concerning shipping operations with ships registered in the Community', SEC (89) 921 FINAL, 3 August.

Department of Transport (1990), 'British Shipping a Vital National Asset', DTp/GCBS, September.

Erdmenger, J. and Stasinopoulos, D. (1988), 'The shipping policy of the EC', Common Market Law Review, Journal of Transport and Economic Policy, September.

European Community Shipowners Associations (1989), Submission on Positive Measures (Commissions Communication COM (89) 266 Final and Document for Information SEC (89) 921 Final).

Fairplay (1990), World Shipping Director, 1990-91, Fairplay Information Systems Ltd.

GCBS (1987), 'The Future of the British Merchant Fleet. An Analysis of Policy Options', December.

GCBS (1989), 'A level playing field for merchant shipping?', May.

GCBS (1990), Joint Government/Industry Working Party on British Shipping: Submission by the GCBS on fiscal issues, HMSO, September.

Government Publication (1988), 'A scheme for Department of Transport assistance for Merchant Navy Officer Training', 3 May.

Green, P. and Tull, D. (1978), Research for Marketing Decisions, 4th Edition.

Hayer, J. (1989), Unpublished MSc Dissertation, Plymouth Polytechnic.

The Independent (1990), 'Time to Steer British Shipping off the Rocks', 14 October.

Joint Working Party (1990), 'British Shipping: Challenges and Opportunities', HMSO, September.

Kay, J.C., Mayer, C. and Thompson, D. (eds) (1986), Privatisation and Regulation

Lloyds List (1990), 'EC Ministers agreed to liberalize cabotage', 19 December.

Lloyds List (1991a), 'EC Cabotage plans face a rethink', 20 February.

Lloyds List (1991b), 'Argument throws cabotage scheme into confusion' 20 March.

Lloyds List (1991c), 'Budget measures will not help preserve UK fleet', 20 March.

Lloyds List (1991d), 'Sea has key role in easing road jams' 30 May.

Lloyds List (1991e), 'Shell to cut tanker fleet by nearly half', 20 June.

Lloyds 1990 Maritime Directory, Lloyds of London Press Ltd.

Lloyds Shipping Economist (1990), 'EC shipping Policy Flagging', February.

Middleton, I. (1989), 'No windows on the wider world', Seatrade Business Review, July/August, pp. 4-7.

Middleton, I. (1986b), 'Juggernaut rolls over Sofeal' Seatrade Business Review, March/April, p. 41.

Moreby, D. and Springett, P. (1989), The UK Shipping Industry Critical Levels Study, British Maritime Charitable Foundation, July.

NUMAST (1991), 'British Shipping - not a sunset industry'.

Odeke, A. (1988), 'Shipping in International Trade Relations'

Scarrot, T. (1989) 'Inside out', Seatrade Business Review, September/October.

Standing Committee on Transport B (1988), 'Official Report', 23 February, c117.

Steele, J. (1986), 'Inside out', Seatrade Business Review, September/October, p.152.

Telegraph (1991), 'Budget aid is called for by NUMAST', NUMAST 24, 12, p. 6.

Telegraph (1991), 'New fleet fall', NUMAST 24, 2.

Tzounas, J.G. (1981), 'In search of a Common Shipping Policy for the EC', Journal of Common Market Studies, XX, 2.

Transport Committee (1988), 'Decline in the UK - Registered Merchant Fleet'.

United Nations (1988), 'Use of Maritime Transport Volume 2. Economic and Social Commission for Asia and the Pacific'.

Appendix 1   Proposal for a Council Regulation

establishing Community ship register and providing for the flying of the Community flag by sea going vessels.

THE COUNCIL OF THE EUROPEAN COMMUNITIES.

Having regard to the Treaty establishing the european Economic Community, and in particular Article 84(2) thereof.

Having regard to the proposal of the Commission.

Having regard to the opinion of the European Parliament.

Having regard to the opinion of the Economic and Social Committee.

Whereas shipping is an indispensable element in trade between the Member States and between Member States and third countries;

Whereas the availability of a high quality and truly competitive fleet depends, on the one hand, on the availability of a maritime infrastructure within the Community including a reserve of national of Member States to serve as seafarers and, on the other hand, a cost level which is competitive;

Whereas the fleet flying Member States' flags has suffered a considerable decline over the years and to the extent that ships have been transferred to third country registers, there has been a severe loss of employment for Community nations;

Whereas the efforts to meet the problem through national measures, inter alia the establishment of second national registers, to which more favourable conditions are attached, tend to disperse the effects of the actions undertaken and risk a distortion of competition;

Whereas it is in the Community interest to aim at a structural development of a fleet of vessels, registered in Member States registers but also identifiable as ships serving Community needs, which comply with the standards of the maritime conventions, and whose crew includes as a minimum a specified number of trained seafarers from Member States;

Whereas this aim cannot be attained without a reduction of the cost level;

Whereas the Commission has developed guidelines for the examination of state aids to be given by the Member States to Community shipping companies;

Whereas the establishment of a Community ship register should serve the purpose of creating a channel through which national efforts can be converged, a pool of Community seafarers and a trade mark guaranteeing shippers a high quality service;

Whereas the Community ship register will be additional to the national register;

Whereas the right to register vessels in the Community register should be reserved for natural and legal persons having a certain link with the Community; whereas, however, this right should also be given under certain conditions to persons having a link with a given third country;

Whereas the vessel to be registered in the Community register should comply with certain conditions; whereas, in particular, the vessel should be and remain registered in a national register; whereas the decisions on the admission to the national register must be taken in compliance with the provisions of the Treaty;

Whereas registration in the Community register should depend on compliance with the safety measures required by the international conventions in this respect;

Whereas the number of trained seafarers from Member States on board of vessels registered in this register should be sufficient to meet future requirements of the Community fleet;

Whereas seafarers from non Community countries on vessels registered in this register should be employed on conditions in conformity with internationally agreed standards, unless otherwise mutually agreed with their representative organizations;

Whereas all seafarers on vessels registered in this register should at least benefit from the social security schemes to which they are entitled in the country where they are resident;

Whereas vessels, while remaining on this register, should be able to transfer between the national registers of Member States without technical hindrance, when they comply with the essential technical requirements to be laid down by the Council.

Whereas the right of free movement under Article 48 of the Treaty as implemented by Council Regulation 1612/68[1] applies to employment of nations of Member States on board vessels registered in the Member States; whereas therefore this right applies to vessels registered in EUROS; whereas, however, the effective exercise of that right may be hindered by differences between qualifications and licences issued in the Member States; whereas it is appropriate to provide for recognition of such qualifications and licences for seafarers for the purposes of employment on board vessels in the Community register subject to minimum requirements laid down by the Council;

Whereas registration in this register should be reflected in the right and obligation to fly the European Flag;

Whereas the Commission should be enabled to adopt implementing provisions concerning the establishment of the register and concerning procedures of registration and deregulation;

Whereas there should be cooperation between the Community register and the national ship registers, including an exchange of information;

[1]OJ No L 257, 19.10.1968, p. 2

Whereas the Member States should take the necessary measures to control and enforce compliance with the provisions of this Regulation;

HAS adopted this regulation:

Section 1 : Scope of the Regulation

Article 1 - Objective

This Regulation provides for :

- the establishment of a Community ship register for sea going merchant vessels;
- the conditions for registration;
- the right to fly the European flag on these vessels in addition to the national flag.

Section 2 : The register, vessel owners and vessels

Article 2 - Establishment of the register.

A Community ship register (hereafter called 'EUROS') is hereby established in which sea going merchant vessels may be registered in addition to their national registration in a Member State.

The Commission shall register when the conditions laid down in Articles 3, 4 and 5 are met. It shall deregister a vessel when it no longer conforms to the provisions of this Regulation.

Article 3 - Persons entitled to have a vessel registered in EUROS.
1) The following may apply for registration of a vessel in EUROS :

a) nationals of the Member States established in a Member State and pursuing shipping activities;
b) a shipping company formed in accordance with the law of a Member State and having its principal place of business in, and effective control exercised within the Community, provided that the majority of the capital of that company is owned by nationals of the Member States or the majority of the board of the company consists of such nations, who have their domicile or usual residence in the Community.
c) nationals of Member States established outside the Community or shipping companies established outside the Community and controlled by nationals of a Member State. If the vessels owned or operated by them are registered in that Member State in accordance with its legislation;

2) For the purpose of this regulation, a natural or legal person meant in paragraph 1 will hereafter be referred to as a 'Community vessel owner';

3) Where it has been agreed between a third country and the Community that registration of vessels in each other's register shall be permitted, the term 'nationals of the Member States' shall, for the purposes only of paragraph 1(a) and (b), include nationals of the third country concerned.

<u>Article 4</u> - Vessels eligible for registration

Eligible for registration in EUROS is any sea going merchant vessel of at least 500 grt, built or under construction, which is already registered in a Member State, and entitled to fly the flag of that Member State and used or to be used in national or international trade for the transport of cargo or passengers or any other commercial purpose, if it fulfils the following conditions:

a) the vessel must be and remain registered in the national ship register for the duration of its registration in EUROS;

b) the vessel must be owned and for the duration of its registration in EUROS remain owned by a person entitled to register a vessel in EUROS, or operated by a Community vessel owner on the basis of a bare boat charter in accordance with the provisions of Article 5;

c) the vessel shall not be more than twenty years old.

<u>Article 5</u> - Bare boat charters

Vessels operated by Community vessel owners on the basis of a bare boat charter may be registered in EUROS during the period of that charter if the following conditions are fulfilled:

1 The vessel is registered as a bare boat chartered vessel in a national ship register of a Member State;

2 the laws of the vessel's initial flag country allow bare boat registration in another country;

3 the consent of the owner of the vessel and of all mortgage creditors for the registration of the bare boat is obtained; and

4 the bare boat charter is duly recorded in the register of the vessel's initial flag country.

<u>Section 3 : Safety, manning and crew</u>

<u>Article 6</u> - Safety

Throughout the period of registration the vessel must be provided with all certificates required by the Member State concerned.

<u>Article 7</u> - Nationality of crew

On vessels registered in EUROS all officers and at least half of the rest of the crew shall be nationals of a Member State.

Trainees do not count towards meeting the requirements above.

<u>Article 8</u> - Wages, working hours and further labour conditions

Wages, working hours and further labour conditions of seafarers, who are not nationals of a Member State, on board vessels registered in EUROS, shall be in accordance with the ILO Wages, Hours of Work and Manning (Sea) Recommendation (No. 109), 1958, subject to any arrangement on collective wages agreed upon with organisations as referred to in Article 9.

Article 9 - Collective wage agreements

1 If Community vessel owners who have registered the vessels which they own or operate in EUROS employ seafarers who are not nationals of a Member State such seafarers may be employed only on the basis of collective wage agreements concluded with trade unions or similar organisations of the country where they are resident.
2 No collective wage agreement may be concluded with a foreign trade union or similar organization on behalf of nationals of a third country if such trade union or organization does not satisfy the conditions of ILO Convention No. 87 concerning the freedom of association and protection of the right to organize.
3 The law of the Member State of registration of the vessel or, if explicitly referred to in the agreement, any other Member State, shall apply to such collective wage agreements. The courts of the Member State concerned shall be competent to hear and determine disputes arising out of such agreements.

Article 10 - Social Security

Without prejudice to Article 13(2)(c) of Council Regulation (EEC) No. 1408/71[1] and unless otherwise mutually agreed at the level of governments of social partners, social security for seafarers on board vessels registered in EUROS shall be the responsibility of the country in which the seafarer is resident unless the legislation of that country expressly provides otherwise, in which case the Member State of registration shall be responsible but in accordance with the legislation of the country of residence.

For the purpose of this provision residence means residence on shore and employment on board a vessel registered in a member state shall not of itself, be considered as being residence in that State.

Article 11

Articles 8, 9 and 10 shall apply subject to any right conferred or obligations imposed by any other Community legislative act except where such act expressly provides otherwise.

Section 4 : Facilities attached to registration in EUROS

Article 12 - Transfer of vessels

Any vessel registered in EUROS and having valid certificates and classification and meeting the essential technical requirements to be laid down by the Council according to the provisions of the Treaty before 1 July 1991, may be transferred to the register of another Member State without the imposition of additional technical requirements.

[2]OJ No. L 149, 5.7.1971, p.2.

<u>Article 13</u> - Recognition of seafarers' qualifications

The qualifications and licences of seafarers who are nationals of a Member State shall be recognised by the competent authorities of each Member State for the purposes of employment on any vessel registered in EUROS, subject to minimum requirements for professional training and experience in the function concerned as required in Directives adopted or to be adopted by the Council, according to the provisions of the Treaty, before 1 July 1991.

<u>Section 5: European flag, port of registration</u>

<u>Article 14</u> - European flag

1 Vessels registered in EUROS are entitled and obliged to fly the European flag in addition to their national flag.
2 Upon registration a certificate conveying the right to fly the European flag will be delivered by the Commission to the applicant for registration.

<u>Article 15</u> - Port of registration

A vessel; registered in EUROS shall bear a relevant identification on its stern under the name of the port of registry in its national register.

<u>Section 6 : Final provisions</u>

<u>Article 16</u> - Implementing measures

The Commission shall, within six months after the adoption of this regulation, adopt the necessary implementing measures concerning the establishment of EUROS, the procedures for registration and reregistration, the form and content of the documents concerned, including the certificate concerning the right to fly the European flag, the form of, and rules governing the flying of, the flag, and the identification of vessels on the register.

<u>Article 17</u> - Cooperation

1 National authorities and the Commission shall assist each other in applying this Regulation and in checking compliance therewith.
2 Within the framework of this mutual assistance they shall communicate to each other the necessary information with respect to registration and deregistration.

<u>Article 18</u> - Transitional period

1 Member states shall, within six months after the adoption of this Regulation and after consultation with the Commission, take the necessary measures to:
- organize effective controls to ensure compliance with the requirements laid down in Sections 3, 3 and 5;
- impose sanctions in case of non compliance with those requirements;
- enable vessels registered in EUROS to exercise the right to fly the European flag.

2 Such measures shall make express reference to this Regulation.

3 Member States shall forthwith communicate to the Commission the measures adopted.

<u>Article 19</u> - Entry into force

This Regulation shall enter into force on 1 January 1991.

This Regulation shall be binding in its entirety and directly applicable in all Member States.

Done at Brussels, ...1989.

For the Council
The President

3 State aid and the shipping industry: A European Community analysis

Paul Hart

Principles

Introduction

In undertaking a study of state aid to maritime industries, it is important to consider a nation's shipping industry in conjunction with its shipbuilding industry. As yet no country has ever maintained a shipbuilding industry without possessing a shipping industry; Beth et al (1984) point out that: 'The development of merchant shipbuilding shows that is a dependable variable of shipping'. There can be no doubt that aids to shipbuilding also have significant repercussions for shipping (Commission of the European Communities 1985). This has long been understood within the European Economic Community (EEC); a seatrade report on EEC shipping in 1978 quotes from an interim report to the European Parliament drawn up for the committee on regional policy, regional planning and transport which states that 'measures taken to support shipyards and shipping companies are often inextricably linked'.

This support has generally taken the form of various subsidies which in an economic context are payments to individuals or businesses by a government for which it receives no products or services in return in an attempt to support the international competitiveness of its shipping and shipbuilding industries (Ademuni - Odeke 1984). In addition there is the need to establish and develop merchant fleets (by reconstruction or renovation) and the need to compensate for special services (such as Scottish Island Ferry Services which are felt to be essential to the economical and social well being of the local community).

Branch (1989) points out that subsidies enable certain governments to save hard currency in that if the cargo is conveyed in a foreign ship it would involve a hard currency outgoing payment. Likewise, the subsidised shipping company carries cargo for other countries and may even operate in a cross trade situation. This earns invisible exports for the maritime country. Consequently the economic assessment of a shipping service will be changed; for example if a service is losing £4 million annually but contributing invisible exports worth £5 million. This might be seen as justifying subsidization. Moreover if the service closed and it cost £6 million in hard currency for foreign carriers to convey such cargo then there would be even more reason for state aid.

MAN - B & W DIESEL (1982) suggest that in the shipbuilding sector subsidies are granted:

1) To shipyards often situated in areas with high or potentially high unemployment.
2) Because yards generate substantial work for contractors.
3) To maintain a certain yard capacity for strategic reasons.
4) Because the industry is export orientated and import substituting.
5) When shipbuilding is chosen as a key sector in the industrial development strategy (it is labour intensive and technological).

If a world existed where international specialization was fully used and no questions of national security were posed then shipbuilding would only be undertaken by those countries most suited by their cost structures and efficiency to operate. However it is one of the economic realities of shipping that political support for national industries decides the fate of shipping companies as much as endeavour, enterprise and hard work (Lloyds List 19 January 1991).

Historical perspective

There is nothing new about the concept of maritime subsidies. An early English reference is cited in Black's law dictionary where a subsidy is described as 'an aid, tax or tribute granted by parliament to the king for the urgent occasions of the kingdom, to be levied on every subject of ability according to the value of his lands'.

As early as the seventeenth and eighteenth centuries subsidies could be seen to be a common feature in British industry. As a result of the protectionism afforded to Britain's merchant fleet, the Dutch lawyer, historian and humanist Hugo Grotius, founded the principles of liberty in the seventeenth century so as to enable free expansion of the Dutch merchant marine (Chrzanowski 1985). Many of the early British steam packet companies were built up by mail subvention and as a result of abundant coal, steel making, industrial innovation, empire preference, monopoly trading and cheap labour the largest and most prestigious fleet in the world was soon developed.

The depression of 1929 lead to widespread subsidies and by 1934 the British Government was compelled to authorize a defence subsidy of £2 million per year until 1937 to protect tramp shipping. Ship losses during the second world war and industrial activity afterwards lead to a sustained growth in demand for shipping services and new ships until the sixties when worldwide shipping capacity became enormous. By the seventies new ships were already being built surplus to requirements. To compound the situation still further, successive oil crises effectively cut demand by one third. By the eighties fleet subsidies were on the increase in a variety of ways and reflected the tendency of nationalism/protectionism adopted by many maritime nations towards fleet development and sustainment. Ships are still being built surplus to requirements, largely because whole communities in Japan, Korea and Europe depend upon orders for their livelihood.

The focus of new building activity has moved increasingly towards the lowest cost or most price amenable procedures, historically from the USA to Europe and since the early seventies from Europe to the Far East. Within Western Europe output fell from 13.4 million gross registered tons (GRT) in 1974, to 3.5 million GRT in 1984 equal to an annual average decline of over fourteen per cent. Loss of direct shipyard jobs in the EEC between 1976 and 1983 exceeded 100,000. Europe's share of overall world output halved from thirty eight per cent in 1974 to nineteen per cent ten years later. Drewry Shipping Consultants (1985) offer the following reasons for this decline:

1 High production costs leading to uncompetitive pricing.
2 Widespread government subsidies propping up uneconomic yards.
3 Insufficient flexibility.
4 Long delivery dates.
5 Inadequate investment.
6 Poor productivity.

As of late however, world shipping has shown a sustained and well founded recovery from the previous decade. Latest statistics from Lloyds Register show that the world fleet has increased to its highest level ever. After a continuous downward trend in the size of the world fleet between 1982 and 1988 it has now increased in size for successive years. At the end of September 1990 tonnage under construction and on order totalled 41.6 million tons - the highest figure since September 1977 (NUMAST 1991a).

However, according to Lloyds Register statistics, the world orderbook fell by 1.8 million gross tons in the final quarter of 1990 and the total tonnage under construction and on order dropped for the first time since 1988. Fearnleys, the Norwegian Shipping analysts said owners are adopting a 'wait and see attitude' in the wake of the Gulf war. The high value of the Japanese Yen and West European currencies, together with concern over rising shipbuilding prices, are also responsible for the fall in orders.

In 1991, Japan still boasts the world's biggest orderbook, with thirty seven per cent of the world total. South Korea is in second place, with twenty one per cent and the unified Germany is in third place with five per cent. The UK orderbook (down to 625,316 gross tons) is the world's thirteenth largest.

Nearly thirty per cent of the 39.8 million gross tons (gt) of ships on order are due to be registered in Liberia. Panama will take the second biggest slice of the orderbook, followed by Norway, the Bahamas, Sweden, the states comprising the ex Soviet Union and Cyprus. The flag states planning the largest additions to their existing fleets are Liberia (11.86 million gt); Panama (6.21 million gt); Norway (2.76 million gt); Japan (1.61 million gt); Denmark (1.53 million gt) and the Bahamas (1.29 million gt). The UK (54 ships of 651,524 gt) stands in thirteenth place (Telegraph April 1991).

Types of subsidy

Maritime subsidies can be grouped into two classes, direct and indirect. Sometimes the difference between the two can be negligible although it is satisfactory to consider direct subsidies as financial aid and indirect subsidies as fiscal relief.

Direct subsidies Financial aid available can be found in the following forms:

• Operational
• Construction
• Modernization

- Depreciation
- Interest/Loans

a) Operational:
   Usually granted to operators in an attempt to place the operating costs of vessels on a parity with foreign competitors. The subsidy is based on the difference between the fair and reasonable cost of insurance, maintenance, repairs not compensated by insurance, wages and subsistence of officers and crews on passenger vessels and the estimated costs of the same items if the vessels were operated under foreign registry.

b) Construction:
   Among traditional maritime nations these are tied to construction in domestic yards and are designed to increase domestic building costs in order to approximate them to those of foreign buildings. All schemes are subject to certain conditions being fulfilled by the beneficiary such as operating the vessel under the national flag for a certain number of years. Constructional subsidies may be a percentage of total building cost or a fixed sum of the constructional cost.

c) Modernization:
   Certain countries in the course of their industrial development have granted aid with a view to the modernization of their fleets and their adaptation to present day competitive conditions. This policy had been strongly applied to France and Sweden's coastal fleets. Modernization subsidies generally fall into three groups: scrap and build, modernization and yard conversion.
   Scrap and build policies are an attempt to encourage owners of older and less competitive ships to scrap them and order new units. The state bears part of the building costs without which the owners would be reluctant to scrap their ships and purchase new. The policy is especially relevant in periods of recession when a number of ships are lying idle. Alternatively it may be quasi permanent to encourage owners to maintain a high fleet quality (Chrzanowski 1985).
   Modernization subsidies are a response to new technological improvements making production techniques introduced only a short time ago obsolete. Countries feel the necessity for state subsidies in order to keep abreast of the changes.
   Yard conversion subsidies are best shown by the example of France where the government supports a programme for the conversion of yards and retraining of employees for other industrial activities. Investment grants of up to twenty per cent of the cost of equipment have been available for the conversion of small and medium sized yards since the decree of 27 December 1960. West Germany has granted credit to port operators to enlarge facilities at interests rates of 5.5 per cent with repayment periods of twelve years.

d) Depreciation:
   The attitudes of fiscal authorities in different countries with regard to the accounting life of a ship vary considerably. Ships may be written off in unchanging amounts over time or in annually decreasing amounts and called actual and accelerated depreciation respectively.
   Depreciation is a reduction in the value of fixed assets as a result of a loss of value by use, decay or corrosion or gradual obsolescence. The annual amount of depreciation of an asset depends upon the original purchase price, estimated useful life and salvage value.
   Accelerated depreciation allocates higher costs to earlier years of an asset's life

when the greatest decrease in resale value normally occurs. It can be used in accordance with tax laws to reduce the overall cost of new capital investments - a widely used policy by British shipbuilders prior to the 1984 Finance Act.

e) Interest and loans:

Many countries offer loans from the government or public financing institutions for new vessel building, purchase or repairs. Conditions vary between countries and frequently between individual loans. All offer some advantage over commercial loans. The prime motive for government intervention is the lack of access to the normal capital markets for some small and medium size owners.

The impact and significance of loans are difficult to assess. Whilst it may be possible to estimate in individual cases the subsidy element of a loan received at less than the market rate of interest, other factors such as prolonged repayment periods, higher borrowing rates with respect to the ship's value and easier access to loan capital are hardly quantifiable.

Individuals, businessmen and governments buy the use of loan monies as do consigners and consignees who pay interest for the use of loan monies because they wish to purchase goods and services in excess of current income. Most maritime nations resort to some form of interest subsidy. In France interest subsidies were designed to bring interest rates for commercial loans down to a minimum of three per cent under certain conditions. In the Netherlands they have been granted in order to furnish credit at reduced rates to both domestic and foreign customers.

Indirect subsidies Fiscal relief of this type usually takes the following forms:

- Investment allowances and grants
- Credit
- Tax benefits
- Customs exemptions
- Seamans' welfare
- Research grants

a) Investment allowances and grants:

Investment allowances, i.e. special allowances for depreciation of more than 100 per cent of the purchase price of a new vessel or asset are granted by many countries, some of which have recently discontinued the scheme and replaced it with investment grants which are assumed to have a similar effect, but are demanding on the public purse. Investment allowances are known under different names and operate as different schemes in differing countries depending upon the accounting systems in existence.

b) Credit:

These can take the form of loans, interest subsidies, loan guarantees, low interest loans, grace periods, long repayment periods and/or credit shares of the total contract price. They are often granted to shipowners for use on new buildings, conversion or resale. There are often different conditions for domestic and export production, the former's conditions generally being the better of the two. The Organisation of Economic Cooperation and Development (OECD) has a general agreement on export credit outlined in a later section.

The deferred credit as a form of investment allowance is sometimes known as loss carrying. In a business, subject to strongly fluctuating trade conditions such as shipping, the permission to carry forward losses in order to deduct these from future profits or to carry back losses to diminish the taxable profit of a previous year may be of considerable significance - the permission to carry forward losses is given in most countries. It should be noted however that provisions may apply in most cases not only to shipping but to all other industries.

c) Tax benefits:
The fiscal system relating to the taxation of shipping may, under certain conditions, have similar beneficial effects for the shipowners as financial assistance. However, fiscal provisions most often apply to income tax liability and consequently will usually be relevant provided that profits are made. With poor profit returns for shipping companies over recent years they have not been able to exploit fully fiscal relief.

d) Customs exemptions:
This is an umbrella name for numerous but related subsidies and bearing different titles in different countries, for example machinery and equipment used in the construction of new ships in a nations' yards may in some circumstances be imported duty free when equivalent goods are not reasonably available from national manufacturers. Alternatively imported materials for incorporation in ships for export is considered as a temporary import and is therefore exempt from customs duty.

e) Research grants:
The rationale behind these grants is that unless the government supports research and development these expenses would be borne by industry thereby diverting valuable investments from direct ploughback. The hope is that money for research and maritime academies to train both shore and seagoing staff will improve efficiency and productivity. The Netherlands Maritime Institute finances part of its maritime research programme with government funds; British shipbuilding research is undertaken by the state run National Physical Laboratory with the government also supporting selected research and development by firms of research associations such as the British Ship Research Association.

The effects of subsidies

Like any other fiscal measure, subsidies indirectly influence trade flows. They tend to increase during recessions as freight rates plunge below the breakeven point. However subsidies are considered 'lesser evil' forms of intervention: they do not directly impose trade barriers, their effects are more easily gauged and they discriminate equally against all foreign shipowners. This is in contrast to flag discrimination which is incompatible with the OECD code of liberalization; financial and fiscal measures are to a certain extent regarded by even the OECD countries as acceptable means of alleviating particular problems of the national shipping sector.

According to Branch (1989) subsidies 'distort the competitive structure of shipping and increase the cost of world shipping services because they permit the use of vessels less efficient and more expensive than is warranted on an economic basis'. To Farthing (1979) subsidies 'bend competitive forces'. These are subjective implications based upon opinion; Eversheim (1958) offers a more objective account of the effects of a subsidy based upon an economic rationale and the reader is referred to that text for further analysis.

47

Policy

Introduction

Chrzwanowski (1985) defines shipping policy as 'a totality of economic, legal and administrative measures by means of which the state influences the position of its national fleet in the national economy and in the international freight market'. Over the years the United Kingdom, Germany, France, Belgium and the Netherlands have all influenced their national fleets in some respect; especially in the face of a declining European community fleet relative to world tonnage - the result of a prolonged recession in world trade, a loss of comparative advantage and the growth of protectionist practices adopted by other countries (Bulletin of the Seventh European Communities Supplement 1985).

Subsidies are just one part of this intervention and what follows is an outline of the policies in existence in the aforementioned countries as well as the governing European Community (EC) and OECD policies.

European Community

The origins of the EC can be found in post war restructuring. During this process many governments accepted that economic and political security would not be guaranteed until countries become so interdependent that conflict between them would be unthinkable (Lloyds Shipping Economist February 1990). Consequently Belgium, France, Germany, Italy, Luxembourg and the Netherlands signed an agreement to manage jointly their coal and steel industries (then seen as the key elements of their economies). The Treaty of Paris established the European coal and steel community, a body which as to serve as the blueprint for the EC, formed by the Treaty of Rome in 1957.

In terms of trade, in 1980 total exports from the EC accounted for thirty four per cent of total world exports; by 1987 they accounted for thirty eight per cent. However, much of this was due to the rapid growth of intra EC trade. If the effects of this are removed the role of the EC in world trade is rather different, in export terms its share rose from 18.7 per cent to 20.5 per cent, in import terms it has fallen from 23.5 per cent to 19.5 per cent.

The geographical pattern of trade has stabilized in recent years; among member states the largest shares are held by Germany, followed by France, the UK and Italy. What is perhaps surprising is the strength of the Netherlands, the fifth largest trader. In terms of trade partners the United States has been the EC's largest for many years, accounting for 16.5 per cent of EC imports and twenty one per cent of exports in 1987. The European Free Trade Association (EFTA) as a bloc constitutes a much larger trading partner than the US. However Japan has become the second largest source of imports (ten per cent) and the fifth largest export destination.

It is a matter of indisputable fact that the EC is inextricably linked with the shipping industry, if only because, as a major trading bloc, it is also a massive user of shipping services (EC shipping 1978). Despite this there has been very little European unity with regard to a common shipping policy. Cafruny (1987) points out that on transport, Article 84, Title 4 in the Treaty of Rome stipulates: 'the provisions of the title shall apply to transport by rail, road and inland waterway. The council may, acting unanimously, decide whether, to what extent, and by what procedure appropriate provisions may be laid down for sea and air transport'.

Consequently issues of a great nationalist interest such as subsidies, cabotage and a European shipping register have not been tackled until very recently. Indeed it was not until the end of 1986 that the first real steps were taken to implement a maritime transport policy. Four regulations were adopted with the aid of promoting free and fair trade:

1 Cargo reservation and similar restriction on trade between EEC countries and with the rest of the world were to be phased out over the next six years, subject to the modified version of the United Nations Conference on Trade and Development (UNCTAD) code of conduct for liner conferences, which the EC endorsed in 1979.
2 The EC's competition rules are to be applied to shipping but will accommodate the conference system in its traditional form.
3 Retaliatory duties can be imposed to counter unfairly low freight rates offered by non EC lines.
4 Counter measures can be taken or threatened if another country restricts the access of EC shipping companies to a particular trade.

Since the adoption of these regulations the Commission has worked to remove subsidies in the shipbuilding sector. Its first attempts began in the relative boom years of the sixties and seventies culminating in a 3rd Directive committed to the removal of all subsidies by the end of 1975. However as European industries fell into catastrophic recession in the mid seventies these intentions were overturned. In the bleakest years between 1981 and 1986 a 5th Directive provided support to minimise the social consequences of industrial collapse whilst at the same time encouraging capital reductions. By the time the 6th Directive took effect in January 1987 substantial community sponsored 'restructuring' had taken place with the EC competition vice president at the time, Leon Brittan, reflecting that EC yards were being increasingly successful at winning orders through strategic specialisation and competitive price. He reiterated the commission's aim eventually to remove subsidies in line with a 'normalization; of the price policies pursued in Japan and South Korea whilst stressing the 'transparency; of EC aid, direct and indirect (Lloyds Shipping Economist February 1990). Consequently the subsidy ceiling was reduced for twenty eight per cent in 1987/88 and twenty six per cent in 1989 to twenty per cent in 1990. The period from 1 January to 1 December 1993 sees the introduction of a 7th Directive subsidy ceiling of thirteen per cent. A ceiling of eleven per cent was favoured by competition commissioner Leon Brittan on the basis of a consultant's report comparing the EC, South Korea and Japanese new building prices, which suggested that the community's most 'efficient' yards could be competitive with subsidies of nine per cent. An additional two per cent was added to compensate the yards for reduced shipbuilding demand during the Gulf crisis. The report was criticized though by both other commissioners and shipbuilding industry representatives on the basis that the prices for five our of the eight vessel types compared were those offered by a Danish yard owned by a major shipowning group - widely believed to be A.P. Moller's Odense yard. Given that fifty three out of the sixty ships built in the last ten years were for the owners the validity of the prices was questioned. The competition directorate however maintained that prices were checked thoroughly.

The subsidy ceiling for vessels with a contract value of less than ECU's ten million and for ship conversion was cut from fourteen per cent to nine per cent.

A spokesman for Sir Leon said he considered thirteen per cent to be 'on the generous side, but one which recognised the political concerns'. The UK Government backed cuts, indeed a figure of ten per cent was preferred. Jim McFall of the UK shipyard group CSEU however opposed the 'drastic' reductions as he called them in the belief that the EC would enter OECD talks in a weaker position in negotiating with Japan and South Korea (Lloyds List 13 December 1990).

The strongest opposition to EC subsidy reductions has come from the Association of Western Europe Shipbuilders. President Werner Fante feels reductions should occur through multilateral negotiations and that the EC's unilateral initiatives were ill advised given the subsidies still enjoyed by the Far Eastern yards.

Organisation for Economic Cooperation and Development (OECD)

When in 1947, the Marshall Plan provided aid for the reconstruction of Europe's economy, a committee of the European countries made a declaration of principles, laying down the criteria for the use of this money for the most advantageous reconstruction of European shipping (Beth et al 1984). A technical subcommittee, from which the maritime transport committee of the OEEC (later the OECD) was formed, declared 'the seaborne traffic between the member countries is based on the principle of free and fair competition. Any infraction of the rule of free movement may result in the profitability of the total available tonnage falling, with increase in transport costs'. (OECD 1963).

This declaration is the basis of the objectives of the maritime transport committee of the OECD and of the liberalization code which Chrzanowski (1985) summarizes into three sections:

i) Governments should apply no pressure on shippers as to their choice of ship to carry their cargoes; this choice should be a matter of normal commercial consideration.

ii) Governments should refrain from discriminating against those of their importers/exporters who wish to 'ship foreign' by imposing import/export licences, refusing to grant them foreign exchange or force them to employ home flag vessels.

iii) Even the government controlled organisations should conduct their business on the basis of normal commercial principles.

The European Community accepts the code but feels that practical compromises have to be made in certain situations where state involvement is required. Thus agreements on export credit for ships were introduced by the OECD and most recently updated in January 1980. These stipulate the maximum terms member countries can grant on loans to non nationals for the purchase of new ships. A maximum of eighty per cent of the contract price can be granted at a minimum eight per cent interest over a maximum repayment period of 8½ years. Payments are normally at six monthly intervals with a maximum gap of twelve months between repayments.

The resolution is a gentlemen's agreement, compliance with which is not obligatory. Most of the major producers within the OECD are, however, signatories to this agreement with the exception of the USA and Spain. Included in the agreement are ship conversions and home owners credit.

It also attempts to maintain a framework of fair competition by discouraging the use of 'other' enticements to potential orderers. Similarly authorization for contravening these terms can be given; especially in the case of aid as long as the OECD is notified at least six weeks beforehand (in very special circumstances only seven days notice need be given). However, the maximum notice is expected to be given to the OECD if a member wishes to contravene the credit terms in order to match a better offer from a non member.

The United Kingdom

The UK has seen its nationally recognised merchant fleet and its role in shipbuilding suffer a general and substantial decline both absolutely and as a proportion of the world fleet.   In the ten years up to 1987 a fleet of 1,400 vessels of over fifty million deadweight (DWT) was reduced to 500 vessels just over ten million DWT. The deep sea fleet reduction over 8½ years was eighty per cent by number and the short sea reduction twenty seven per cent by number. At the start of 1991 there were just 310 ships of 3.8 million deadweight (DWT). In the last fifteen years the number of seafarers on British ships has fallen from more than 70,000 to less than 18,000 today (Telegraph April 1991). In the liner sector, the remaining general cargoliners were replaced by large containerships and by an increasing number of chartered in medium sized container ships. There has been a withdrawal from tanker, bulk carrier and refrigerated cargo tramp vessel ownership.

Fifteen years ago more than half the UK fleet was less than five years old - below the average for the world fleet. Today not only is the UK fleet much older at 13.7 years but the world average is 12.7 years (Lloyds List 19 February 1991).

Running parallel to the decline in the British fleet has been the growth in flags of convenience (FOCs) such as Panama and Liberia which were initially deplored by British shipowners who later on 'flagged out' in large numbers.

Various governments have paid little attention to this trend; the shipping policy division of the Department of Transport in advice given to the Select Committee looking into the decline of the British Merchant Navy considered that

> Any initial adverse economic effects on the shipping sector, resulting from the transfer of vessels away from the UK register will be offset by economic adjustments elsewhere in the economy, which leave the overall effect of employment and output largely unaffected. Indeed the sale of loss making vessels to overseas interests and the redeployment of resources into more profitable industries will help to improve the overall performance of the economy. Any case for assistance to the shipping industry therefore, must be strategic; it has no compelling economic base.

a) Fiscal regime Before the introduction of the 1984 Finance Act the fiscal regime for ships owned by British resident companies was fairly simple. There was a depreciation allowance of 100 per cent in the first year of a ship's operation, interest was deductible and the remainder, if any, was subject to corporation tax at fifty two per cent. The first year allowance could be carried forward by way of tax loses, but it was obviously more valuable to use it as soon as possible and a number of arrangements were made to achieve this. These included company mergers e.g. between property companies with good profits and small tax allowances and shipping companies in opposite circumstances, and leases by which the ownership of the vessel was taken by another company, for example a bank which was able to take full and immediate advantage of the 100 per cent allowance, the benefits of which were duly shared between partners to the deal. (Goss, in a memorandum to the House of Commons Transport Committee report on the decline in the UK registered merchant fleet 1988).

The 1984 Act introduced a general series of reforms into corporate taxation. this

51

followed a general governmental philosophy of no longer believing that favourable tax allowances stimulate overall investment for shipping. These changes involved the substituting of a twenty five per cent reducing balance depreciation allowance for the 100 per cent first year allowance and reducing the rate of corporation tax (eventually) to thirty five per cent. The tax deductibility of interest was continued but its value was reduced by the fall in the rate of corporation tax. These changes have the effect of making companies better off at the higher rates of profit and worse off at the lower ones. Since the abolition of depreciation allowances in 1984 budget investment in UK shipping has fallen rapidly. An attempt by the UK Government to stimulate investment by allowing business expansion schemes (BES) to apply to shipping ventures has met with limited success in terms of projects launched and response of the investing public. Part of this is due to the fact that BES schemes are limited both in terms of the amount of funding which can be raised and on the length of charters that can be secured (Lloyds Shipping Economist April 1989). British resident companies employing British seamen find themselves paying more than competitors (usually FOCs) due to social security, pension contributions, study leave and pay. In addition FOC operators pay wages as 'gross remuneration; i.e. without any deductions at all therefore income tax has become a burden on British ship employers as have their social security and pension contributions. The UK Centre for Maritime Policy Studies has stated that personal taxation and social security costs have become an important elements in the competitive cost equation between traditional maritime nations and flags of convenience. The Centre points to the example of several nations in the European Community which have recognized the importance of their effects, adding that it is now the practice of the EC to approve schemes for positive measures to put the EC seafarer tax and social security structures on a par with those outside the EC. The anomalies and complexities of the UK system, it says, have a detrimental effect on employment, severely inhibiting the recruitment and retention of British seafarers.

In the shipbuilding sector the UK's share of European and global output has been declining too. The industry has suffered badly from union problems and restrictive practices, which have tended to result in the late delivery of over budget vessels. Yards have generally lacked the capital and labour relations needed for installing more efficient methods that would enable them to achieve on time delivery and thus compete with low labour cost yards abroad. In line with other heavy industries governmental policy has attempted to balance commitments to employment while allowing the restructuring of the industries concerned. Since 1979 the balance has shifted to the latter; the government has sought to disentangle itself from industry, on one hand privatizing anything profitable and on the other tightening the conditions for government aid and cutting back on assistance given to older industries.

b) Direct subsidies From 1 January 1991 the UK has reduced the maximum level of subsidy for merchant shipbuilding from twenty per cent to thirteen per cent in line with the EC Seventh Shipbuilding Directive, agreed by ministers in Brussels last December. This also covers small ships, the definition of which has been changed to increase the maximum price to £13 million. This reflects the EC increase of maximum value from ECU 6 million to ECU 10 million. The ceiling for subsidies for these small ships is now nine per cent. The subsidy levels operating within the UK's shipbuilding intervention fund were announced by Edward Leigh, Parliamentary Under Secretary of State for Industry and Consumer Affairs. There is considerable feeling amongst those in the UK that the Directive should have gone further. Nick Granger, Managing Director of the

Shipbuilders' and Shiprepairers' Association feels that 'if there were no subsidies we would be in with a chance'. (Fairplay 10 January 1991).

c) Indirect subsidies The Export Credit Guarantee Department (ECGD) lends to foreign owners, guaranteeing a commercial bank loan at a fixed rate of interest, the difference between this and market interest rates being paid by the government. The terms available amount to eighty per cent of contract price over 8½ years at 7.5 per cent interest. When guarantee premiums and bank charges are included, the effective interest rate equates to the OECD rate of eight per cent. If the foreign content of the vessel is high the size of the loan is reduced. Similarly, if the contract value is under £1 million the repayment period can vary from five to seven years. Seventeen equal payments will normally be made at six monthly intervals, the first being six months after delivery.

The government provides guarantees to commercial banks which supply loans to domestic owners at subsidized interest rates, the difference between this rate and the market rate of interest being made up by the government. Loans are provided up to eighty per cent of the contract price at 7.5 per cent over a maximum repayment period of 8½ years.

Germany

The shipping policy of the Federal Republic of Germany has been shaped by post Second World War circumstances. Massive aid was required from the government in order to reconstruct the Merchant Navy. 1950 saw the 'Act on loans for the construction and purchase of merchant ships' and the 'Act on modification of the income tax act and corporation tax act' which arranged interest free loans and subsidies for shipbuilding to be set off against taxable income as business expenses. In the following years West Germany operated almost all imaginable forms of subsidy with a total value of DM2.58 billion aid for the period between 1945 and 1980. This aid has been typical of the governmental assistance that has boosted the West Germany economy and made it so strong.

In the mid 1980s the economy went through a period of stagnation as the government prioritized the tackling of inflation, through a tough monetary policy, over growth. This lead, at the beginning of 1991, to Guenther Krause, the Transport Minister cancelling the payment of DM140 million earmarked in the draft budget for direct financial aid to German shipowners. This year the financial squeeze in Bonn is tighter than ever before, with huge sums required to handle the restoration and reorganization of industries in East Germany in addition to the contribution to the Gulf war. Owners are fighting the decision because the direct aid, introduced in 1987 when the government decided to separate aid to builders and owners, forms an integral part of the package devised to increase the competitiveness of the German flag fleet and provide incentives to stop owners from 'flagging out' (Lloyds List 9 February 1991). The package has included, since Spring 1989, a second register that gives greater cost flexibility to owners by allowing them to hire foreign seafarers with lower wages than paid to German seamen. The package also includes some tax breaks but the government has not reduce1xor eliminated the existing business tax as demanded by the owners.

The shipbuilding sector historically has been in a strong position both within Europe and world economies. Although costs are high and direct subsidies are low, yards have benefited from technological sophistication, flexibility, quality workmanship and strict adherence to delivery dates. A large scale restructuring of the industry has been undertaken and yards claim they can be the most competitive in the world given a significant reduction in protectionist measures overall.

Consequently since 1975 the West German shipbuilding workforce has fallen from 75,000 to about 30,000 with the closure of well known yards like A.G. Weser in Bremen and Howaldtswerke Deutsche Werfts' (HDW) Hamburg facility. Capacity and resources, according to the survivors, are now at the minimum necessary to meet projected market developments and to maintain hard won capabilities in sophisticated new building sectors. The industry is based on three major groupings, largely forged from 1986 to 1988, which together account for around sixty per cent of the overall capacity: the Bremen based Vulkan Group, the Kiel based HDW Group (seventy five per cent owned by a public sector steel enterprise) and the Hamburg based Blohm and Voss.

The government has followed a policy of reduced subsidization believing that too much state intervention erodes competition. Despite limited (direct) aid from Federal sources assistance may be boosted at local level. The coastal states of Schleswig Holstein (controlling the remaining twenty five per cent of HDW), Bremen and Lower Saxony have all financially assisted local yards in the 1980s.

a) Direct subsidies From 1965 to 1987 a 12.5 per cent state aid scheme was available to West German owners provided they ordered ships in West Germany and kept them under the country's flag for eight years. Between 1987 and 1990 a three year subsidy programme existed and p1xvided up to twenty per cent assistance and totalled DM1 billion. In 1990 the government decided not to extend the programme as a result of a healthy national orderbook situation. The government will still spend DM450 million on easing the situation in shipbuilding in 1991 (in the current year the subsidy stands and 9.5 per cent) with assistance for interest payments and help in completing foreign orders (the industry has demanded DM800 million). This indirect foreign aid consists of:

b) Export credit assistance Loans are being provided by the Kreditanstalt fuer Wiederaufbau (KFW) in compliance with OECD guidelines. The bank is eighty per cent government owned, the remaining twenty per cent being held by the local states.

Werner Fante, managing Director of the Association of German Shipbuilding and Marine Technology believes the subsidy policies of other shipbuilding nations necessitates German assistance and protection but he would support lower subsidies provided other countries reduced theirs. In his opinion a unilateral subsidy cut would reduce German influence on EC policies.

German shipbuilding must be seen in the context of reunification and the uncertainties this has brought into the structure, profitability and productivity of the industry (Lloyds Shipping Economist, May 1990). In shipbuilding, as in other former East German industries, it has become clear that the restructuring needed to enable these industries to find their niche in a world market is even more extensive than at first thought. Although reunification catapulted Germany into the number three position after Japan and south Korea this holds true for capacities only, it reveals nothing about the competitiveness of the newly joined shipbuilding industries. The Eastern yards will have to find clients on the international market where they were barely present in the past. The East German capacities were created for there major purposes - to meet the regime's prestige needs, to meet reparations demands by the Soviet Union and to collect convertible currencies by offering newbuildings at dumping prices (Lloyds List 22 January 1991). Of the 1.6 million compensated gross tons in the East German orderbooks, seventy five per cent are for the Soviet Union. Recent reports (Lloyds List 11 February 1992) suggest that the management board are charged with the traumatic task of restructuring the industry were likely to recommend the cancellation of some orders on account of projected losses of DM1.8 billion. The board chairman Dr Eckart van Hooven made it clear that a major shrinking process was inevitable although he felt the government would have to authorize payment of the Soviet orders if the industry was to survive the transition from a command to a market economy.

The new EC 7th Directive contains a special declaration recognizing the particular problems faced by former East German yards and contains a commitment that the yards will be brought into the full EC shipbuilding framework as soon as possible.

France

France occupies a central position in Western Europe bordering on six countries. To the north are Belgium and Luxembourg, to the east Germany, Switzerland and Italy and to the south, Spain. France is the fourth largest OECD economy: behind the United States, Japan and Germany but ahead of Britain. The French are very conscious of the role shipping has to play in its economy both regionally and nationally and historically there has always been a strong element of flag protection in French shipping. Strict cabotage is applied and there is a degree of protection in trade between France and its overseas territories. Decrees of 1921 rule that preference must be given to government trade; since 1928 two thirds of petroleum imports and since 1936 forty per cent of coal imports have to be carried in vessels flying the French flag.

a) Direct subsidies Between 1961 and 1969 subsidies were available to reduce o1xrating costs, since then they have been granted mainly to help with fitting out. In September 1989 there was a cool response from French shipowners to the long awaited announcement of state financial support fro the French merchant marine. They feel the level of funding available will not be enough to protect the competitive position of the French flag operators in the 1990s and that 'flagging out' will continue. They blame much of their troubles on laws introduced as far back as 1680 - obliging owners to hire totally French crews and make sizeable contributions to pension funds and the like. France's national line Compagnie General Maritime (CGM) has estimated that it costs $2,000 per day more to operate a containership under the French flag than under foreign flags, due primarily to the high cost of social security (Lloyds Shipping Economist, November 1989). Between 1982 and 1989 the French fleet fell from 17.3 to less than 6.3 million deadweight tonnes. The recently announced (1990) package of government support involves the provision of FF2 billion (£300 million) of state aid over a five year period providing vessels remain under the French flag, specific employment is guaranteed and there is some form of modernization and acquisition. In the first year FF443 million was provided, FF100 million for specific modernization projects, tax concessions of FF90 million and FF26 million to raise crewing levels. Amongst those who will benefit are CGM and Brittany Ferries who will receive $17 million and £2.6 million respectively for 1991.

This level of support, approved by the socialist government of Prime Minister Michel Rocard is interesting in light of a report presented to the government in May 1989 by Jean Yves Le Drian, mayor of Lorient, who was commissioned twelve months beforehand to recommend long term policies to enhance the competitiveness of French shipping companies in the 1990s. He proposed a package of measures supported by

FF560 million per year1xn state funding. The French Minister of the Sea, Jacques Mellick acknowledged that the aid was only seventy per cent of that recommended by Le Drian but was pleased it was not lower. Claude Abraham, President of CGM and chairman of the Central Council of French Shipowners (CCAF) supported the measures outlined but double the level of state aid was needed, he felt, in light of the problems shipping faced. The CCAF's UK counterpart, the General Council of British Shipping, cast envious glances however at the French announcement (Lloyds Shipping Economist October 1989).

Shipbuilding in France is dominated by two major groups - Chantiers du Nord et de la Mediterranee (NORMED) with two yards (at Dunkirk and la Seyne) and Althom Atlantique with one at St Nazaire. French yards tend to specialize in more sophisticated vessels such as cruise ships, car ferries, chemical carriers and gas carriers. In February the St Nazaire yard signed a deal with the Malaysian state oil company Petronas reputedly worth £1.3 billion for five LNG carriers in the face of intense competition from Japan. The coup is very much in contrast to the last two decades, when France has seen its importance in shipbuilding eroded with the government experiencing the dilemma of wanting to reduce costs in an effort to be more competitive, yet at the same time safeguarding the maximum number of jobs (many yards are in depressed areas) and maintain the industry for strategic reasons. The net result has been that compromise has been the chosen strategy - slowly reducing the workforce through early retirement and temporary lay offs. In addition wages rises at home, social considerations and low vessel prices on world markets have forced the French to raise the building subsidies, in particular construction and investment subsidies in line with EC directives and export/domestic credit assistance on OECD terms.

The shipbuilders themselves have expressed their position clearly in a communique issued in September 1989 by the Chambre1xyndicate des Constructeurs de Navires (CSCN) who recognize that state subsidies are necessary to preserve shipbuilding in certain regions but are critical of those nations which profess to being unsubsidized but nevertheless require respective state support once accumulated debts mount after successive years of signing loss making contracts (Lloyds Shipping Economist October 1989).

Belgium

Belgium, frontiering with the Netherlands to the north, France to the south west and Germany and Luxembourg to the east has one of the most open economies in the world, reflecting the country's geographical position and the importance of foreign trade. The Belgian Government has always maintained a fairly detached attitude to the merchant fleet due to its relative insignificance as an employer, compared to heavy industry. Its shipbuilding sector is, however fundamentally weak. High production costs and the reservation of government loans exclusively for domestic flag operators has tended to deny domestic yards the ability to compete for orders from abroad; in the past the trend of Belgian shipbuilding was for yards to build ships for operation by their own associates or subsidiary companies, although small vessels (push tugs, pusher barges and wagon ferries) have been built for developing countries including Egypt, the Sudan, Tanzania and Nigeria (Drewry 1985).

The main shipbuilding company in Belgium is Boelwerf, saved from bankruptcy in 1987 by the government and subsequently forced to cut staff by forty per cent. In 1990 it registered a positive cash flow and a small profit (Motor Ship January 1991).

Although there is said to be no official policy on shipbuilding, direct grants or subsidies, there is a special loan system dating back to 1948. Chiefly of benefit to owners the system has nevertheless been of considerable benefit to the yards. Funding is provided by a special government fund and the Societe Nationale du Credit a l'Industrie. Loans are p1xvided up to seventy per cent of the cost of the newbuilding at interest rates of 4.25 per cent per annum for thirteen to fifteen years with the interest rates adjusted every five years. To obtain the loan the vessel must fly the Belgian flag with a maximum complement of Belgian crew. If the vessel is sold within five years all subsidies must be repaid.

Export Credit Assistance generally follows OECD guidelines. There has been particular aid to developing countries typically granted over twenty years at zero per cent to two per cent interest per annum with a maximum grace period of ten years.

The government is currently assessing alternative systems to bring Belgium in line with other countries benefiting from direct EC subsidies; Boelwerf is reasonably confident that direct subsidies will be approved and that they will work in combination with the existing home credit scheme.

The Netherlands

One of the world's most densely populated countries, the Netherlands, is a small state with over half its land area lying below sea level. Nearly sixty per cent of the working population is engaged in transport, trade and associated services. Three of Europe's most important navigable rivers, the Rhine, Maas and Scheldt enter the North Sea from Holland making it a major gateway for overseas trade for much of the north and central parts of the continent.

There is a long history of shipbuilding, repair and conversion in the Netherlands although in the last few decades the country has had to witness the spectacle of its building capacity being reduced. Today there are 131 vessels of over 4,000 GRT employing 1,928 seafarers and 270 vessels of less than 4,000 GRT employing 1,760 seafarers.

Dutch yards have been restructuring since 1976 when the first stage of the government shipbuilding policy began. Since that date there have been significant reductions in manpower and capacity. Significant injections of state aid has helped some yards to survive although the g1xernment is determined not to bail out shipbuilding companies indefinitely - 1983 saw the collapse of Rijn Schelde Verolme (RSV) formerly the largest shipbuilding and repair concern in the country, 1984 saw the demise of NSM while Amsterdam's only large yard ADM went bankrupt in February 1985. The yards believe that their future survival lies in specialization and it is unlikely the country will ever again build large merchant ships. In 1984 the yards claimed that productivity had improved by sixteen per cent over the last couple of years, putting the country at the head of the European productivity table and second worldwide behind Japan.

The largest shipbuilding company in the Netherlands is now Van de Giessen-de-noord, a company currently specializing in building ferries although cuts in government subsidy to the yard in the Spring of 1985 forced the cancellation of a £50 million contract.

Aid to domestic owners is available in the form of:

Tax credit schemes: where 12.5 per cent of the investment (less premiums) is deducted from the tax bill. If the vessel is sold within eight years of the delivery the owner must pay back the grant. Furthermore if the investment generates a loss to the owner the grant is paid to him in cash by the taxation authorities.

Investment premium schemes: A premium of 2.5 per cent is given over five years provided there is a minimum number of Dutch seamen employed.

Export credit assistance: The government pays interest support of up to two per cent on eighty per cent of the contract price for a period of 8½ years with a possible 0.5 per cent in addition, for contracts under DFL 5 million. This compares poorly with several other competitor countries which subsidize their industries down to OECD minimum interest levels of eight per cent.

Domestic credit assistance: Loans are available under OECD guidelines although interest rates are based on commercial rates with an interest subsidy of up to two per cent for ocean going vessels (Drewry 1985).

The Netherlands has said it will not allow any form of subsidies towards ship conversion work and has expressed concern about the implications of continuing any subsidies. The Deputy Managing Director of Holland's Wilton-Fijenoord yard says 'within the EC the ship conversion industry is in the black. It is ridiculous to subsidize such an industry. It doesn't need any help from government. Without subsidies there could be fair competition' (Fairplay 10 January 1991). He is concerned that the German yards which presently account for a major part of the conversion work will increase in their domination of the market, particularly as the German government has said that it will continue to allow its yards to take advantage of the EC's 7th Directive. However, he remains optimistic as he feels that as a result of labour and raw material costs the Netherlands is about ten per cent cheaper than Germany.

Opinion

Introduction

This section deals with the viewpoints of those parties in the UK with a vested interest in subsidies and their effects, in particular shipowners/managers, shipbuilders/repairers and the maritime organizations representing them.

A survey was undertaken in order to gauge this opinion; organizations such as the General Council of British Shipping (GCBS), National Union of Marine Aviation and shipping (NUMAST) and the National Union of Seamen (NUS) were approached for their official perspectives on the relevant issues. These organizations were chosen as they represent the employers and employees of the British Merchant Fleet. In addition 100 postal questionnaires were sent out to various shipping companies, builders and organizations.

Organizational opinion

All of the organizations approached were keen to dispel the notion that they were seeking subsidies or 'handouts' but rather that they were trying to obtain fiscal incentives to reverse a declining merchant fleet, dwindling in numbers as a result of 'flagging out' and insufficient newbuilding. The cure for these symptoms was generally felt to be the reintroduction of a 100 per cent tax allowance on capital investment in new tonnage and the abolition of seafarers' tax and national insurance contributions.

General Council of British Shipping (GCBS) The GCBS has been very vocal on the subject of fiscal support from the government during 1990 and 1991, the culmination of which was the 1991 UK Budget submission. Last May GCBS president Lord Sterling announced that the government had agreed to establish a joint working party to look into the future of the industry, chaired jointly by himself and the then Transport Secretary Cecil Parkinson. The conclusions presented in September 1990 were that British shipping was a 'vital national asset'. (UK Department of Transport/GCBS, 1990).

The GCBS recommended that if British shipping was to seize the commercial opportunities recognized by the working party and thus benefit not only the general economy but other maritime related industries then a 100 per cent ship allowance should be introduced. This would help rebuild the ageing fleet and create flexibility in company cash flow when it is needed most - to invest in new ships when interest payments are highest. The allowance would make the return on investment in new or second hand ships far more attractive to owners who, it say, need the ability either to write off all their investment in year one or to spend it against years when sufficient profits are available. In net present values (assuming the Treasury's eight per cent discount factor) the introduction of a ship allowance would be equivalent to a six per cent discount in the present (1990) price of a ship. The practical benefit to a shipping company would be even greater as it would apply a high discount factor in view of the risk element and the need to raise funds on the commercial market.

The Council additionally felt that income tax and employers national insurance contributions are a burden and should be removed to make the employment of British seamen in significant numbers affordable.

With the help of a regulatory and fiscal package the GCBS said that shipping's £5 billion contribution to the UK economy could be doubled to £10 billion by the end of the decade. However, if matters are allowed to continue as they are then 'a further decline of the red ensign could be irreversible' particularly in passenger and liner trades (GCBS 1991).

The joint working party, in conclusion, gave five recommendations it considered necessary to secure a better future for the industry:

a) The speeding up and simplification of technical procedures and regulations concerning the Department of Transport registration requirements.
b) The introduction of more flexibility into the rules governing the nationality of officers on British ships.
c) Allowing chartered in vessels to be registered in the UK and vice versa.
d) The vigorous pursuit in Brussels of the liberalization of cabotage and a more competitive financial environment.
e) The raising of the profile of marine training and the urgent pursuit of an action plan for change.

The National Union of Marine and Shipping Transport Officers (NUMAST) and the National Union of Seamen (NUS) Whilst the unions support much of the working party's findings, some of the aforementioned recommendations met with adverse comment. This was especially true for point two with NUMAST believing that British officers offer profitability through quality and that cost cutting would be best achieved by fiscal incentives. In a letter to the Chancellor of the Exchequer, NUMAST General Secretary John Newman expressed his and many others' belief that

> The retention of a pool of professional seafarers would ensure the UK maintains its leading maritime safety record. It would provide the corps of skilled and loyal

seafarers needed to keep our ships sailing at a time of national crises and it would ensure that the UK's maritime related industries continued to be supplied with the seafaring expertise they need to prosper. (Telegraph March 1991).

Survey opinion The objectives of the questionnaire were threefold:

a) To establish operators' perceptions of competing countries.
b) To determine the level of respondent support for subsidies and their format.
c) To quantify any desire for legislative change.

With the aforementioned objectives in mind a series of twenty questions was formulated with ease of reading, understanding and consequently answering being prime considerations. The answering procedure consisted of the simple ticking of boxes with the facility to expand and comment where appropriate. All of the questions (listed in Figure 1) had underlying intentions and reasons for inclusion as follows:-

Question 1: To establish who the respondents were in terms of four employment categories and their proportion of the total responses.

Question 2: To determine respondents' underlined perceptions of their operating position in relation to specified countries. As a consequence this question was placed at the very beginning of the questionnaire as it was felt that having answered a number of questions on subsidies, answering this question at the end would have made respondents attempt to justify their answers by exaggerating their response.

Question 3 and 4: These were included to give an early indication of whether there was a desire to see trade liberalized or whether companies preferred to operate under the cloak of protectionism.

Questions 5 to 10: This group of questions were designed primarily to achieve the second survey objective; are subsidies desirable? If so, for what reasons? And in what form?

Question 11: This question was used to judge whether the operators agree with the economic principles and effects.

Questions 12 to 15: This section determined feelings on the administration of subsidies and the form any changes should take.

Questions 16 to 20: The third questionnaire objective was satisfied through this group of questions.

Question 21: Space was provided for respondents to express any comments or opinions on the questionnaire design or subject matter.

Analysis

One hundred postal questionnaires were sent out to companies and organisations within the shipping and shipbuilding industries, 40 being sent to shipowners/managers, 36 to shipbuilders/repairers and 24 to organizations. These were selected from Fairplay World Shipping Directory in alphabetical order and using UK addresses.

There were 57 responses; 42 respondents completed questionnaires whilst 15, for varying reasons, felt they could not answer the questions. Of the positive responses 48 per cent were owners, 31 per cent builders and 21 per cent organizations. This is in similar proportions to those sent out although with nearly half the responses being from owners the results will be influenced somewhat.

Shipping Subsidy Questionnaire

1   In which of the following lines of business are you involved?

   shipowners/managers
   shipbuilders/repairers
   maritime organisation
   other (please state)

2   How do you feel you operate in relation to the following countries?

	At a disadvantage	On equal terms	At an advantage
France			
Belgium			
Holland			
Germany			

3   Which of the following would you rather see?

   The opening up of trade in foreign countries.
   The introduction of restrictive counter measures

4   Do you feel the UK should operate a restrictive access policy to its cabotage trade?

   Yes   No

5   Are you in favour of subsidies to support the international competitiveness of this country's shipping industry?

   Yes   No   (go to Q7)

	Yes	No
To develop/protect fleets?		
To remedy financing problems?		
To compensate social services?		
To ensure national security?		
For other reasons? (please state)		

....

....

7 Are you in favour of subsidies to support the international competitiveness of this country's shipbuilding industry?

Yes ☐   No ☐   (go to Q12)

8 If you answered Yes to question 7 do you feel subsidies should exist:-

	Yes	No
To protect local and subcontracted employment?		
To maintain capacity for strategic reasons?		
For key sectors in industrial development strategy?		

Other reasons (please state)

....

9 Which of the following types of subsidy are you in favour?

Direct		Indirect	
operational		investment allowances/grants	
construction		credit	
modernization		tax benefits	
depreciation		customs exemptions	
interest/loans		seamans welfare	
		research grants	

10 Do you feel subsidies should be granted to:

coastal vessels engaged in domestic trade ☐
vessels operating on international services ☐

11 How far do you agree with the following statements on subsidies? (Enter 1-5 using the following scale:)

1 - strongly disagree; 2 - disagree; 3 - impartial; 4 - agree; 5 - strongly agree

they destroy commercial freedom

they increase efficiency and competitiveness

they bend competitive forces

they inflate capacity

they promote nationalism

they increase the cost of world shipping services

12 Do you feel subsidies should be discretional?

Yes ☐   No ☐

13 Do you feel subsidy reductions/increases should occur:-

either: through multilateral negotiations

or: as an EEC unilateral initiative

14 Should subsidies be given to British companies operating under foreign flags?

Yes ☐   No ☐

15 Do you favour subsidies over greater forms of intervention such as trade barriers?

Yes ☐   No ☐

16 Would you be in favour of a return to pre-1984 agreements where shipowners were allowed to offset 100% of a ship's value against profits for the first year?

Yes ☐   No ☐

17 Do you agree with the OECD understanding on ship export credits?

Yes ☐   No ☐

18 Do you feel shipowners should be able to retain profits in a tax free reserve against future investment in ships?

Yes ☐   No ☐

19 Do you agree with the UK corporation tax rate?

Yes ☐   No ☐

20 Do you feel the government should give more favourable rates of:-

seafarers income tax   ☐
employers national insurance ☐

21 Please state any relevant comments or opinions:-

....
....

Figure 1 Shipping Subsidy Questionnaire

The respondents generally felt they were operating at a disadvantage to operators in the four other nations, more so the shippers than the builders probably as a result of the progress made by the EC directives on subsidy reductions to shipbuilding. If we study Figures 2 to 6 we can see how the countries compare. Respondent percentages are shown for the three categories disadvantaged, on equal terms and at an advantage for each nation.

The two countries with the highest levels of subsidy, France and Germany, were viewed by the operators as having foreign counterparts who were much better off. Seventy one per cent of respondents felt they were at a disadvantage to French competition and seventy six per cent to Germany. With regard to Belgium and the Netherlands the majority of builders (sixty two per cent) feel they were on an equal footing although the owners still believe they are disadvantaged. Sixty seven per cent of all the organizations felt at a disadvantage of all four countries.

So, with general dissatisfaction over parity of operating conditions in existence how would the respo ndents like to see the playing field levelled?

There was overwhelming support (eighty eight per cent) for liberalizing trade in foreign countries as opposed to twelve per cent who would rather see the introduction of restrictive counter measures by the UK. Only seventeen per cent believed the UK should operate a restrictive access policy to its cabotage trade. NUMAST's position on this issue is quite clear; they believe that there should be free trade in coastal services (except in agreed 'special cases; such as remote island links) and therefore would not wish to see unilateral UK cabotage restrictions. However, the union was dissatisfied with progress on eliminating existing cabotage restrictions, particularly within the EC and felt that 'if decisive action is not forthcoming we would then wish to see the UK adopting certain restrictions to access to British cabotage trade as a retaliatory measure'. (NUMAST 1991b).

It is clear then that operators want to see trade opened up but realize that this is not imminent and therefore feel it is necessary to protect themselves.

Among the comments expressed the following four were typical responses:

To enable us to compete on equal terms...would prefer that there were no subsidies anywhere.

Comparative subsidies to compensate for hidden subsidies in other countries.

Subsidies are a poor alternative - their only justification is they are better than the current approach which is do nothing and see the death of British shipping.

Subsidies/protection/cabotage is practised to varying degrees by most maritime nations except the British. It is pointless to continue our lone stand position.

As a result it was not surprising to find that despite 88 per cent in favour of opening up trade, 25 per cent and 50 per cent said they were in favour of subsidies to support the international competitiveness of this country's shipping and shipbuilding industries respectively. In particular, those in favour of subsidies to shipping felt they should be administered as follows:-

- To develop/protect fleets   :   77 per cent
- To remedy financial problems   :   77 per cent
- To compensate social services   :   27 per cent
- To ensure national security   :   59 per cent

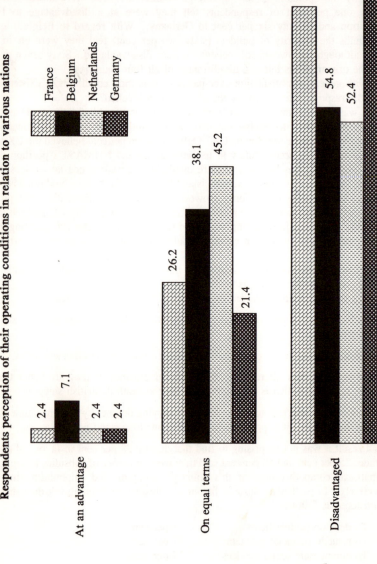

Figure 2

Respondents perception of their operating conditions in relation to various nations

France
Belgium
Netherlands
Germany

At an advantage
2.4
7.1
2.4
2.4

On equal terms
26.2
38.1
45.2
21.4

Disadvantaged
71.4
54.8
52.4
76.2

Figure 3
Category of respondent – France

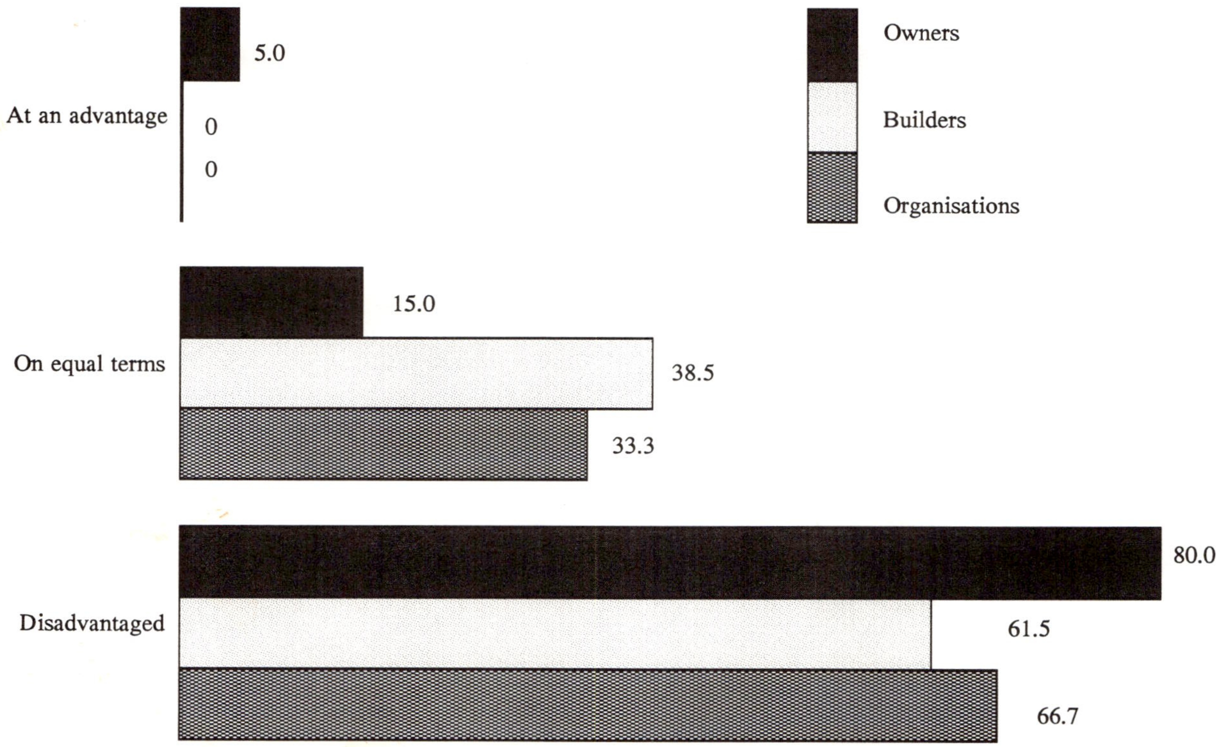

Legend:
- Owners
- Builders
- Organisations

At an advantage
- Owners: 5.0
- Builders: 0
- Organisations: 0

On equal terms
- Owners: 15.0
- Builders: 38.5
- Organisations: 33.3

Disadvantaged
- Owners: 80.0
- Builders: 61.5
- Organisations: 66.7

Figure 4
Category of respondent – Belgium

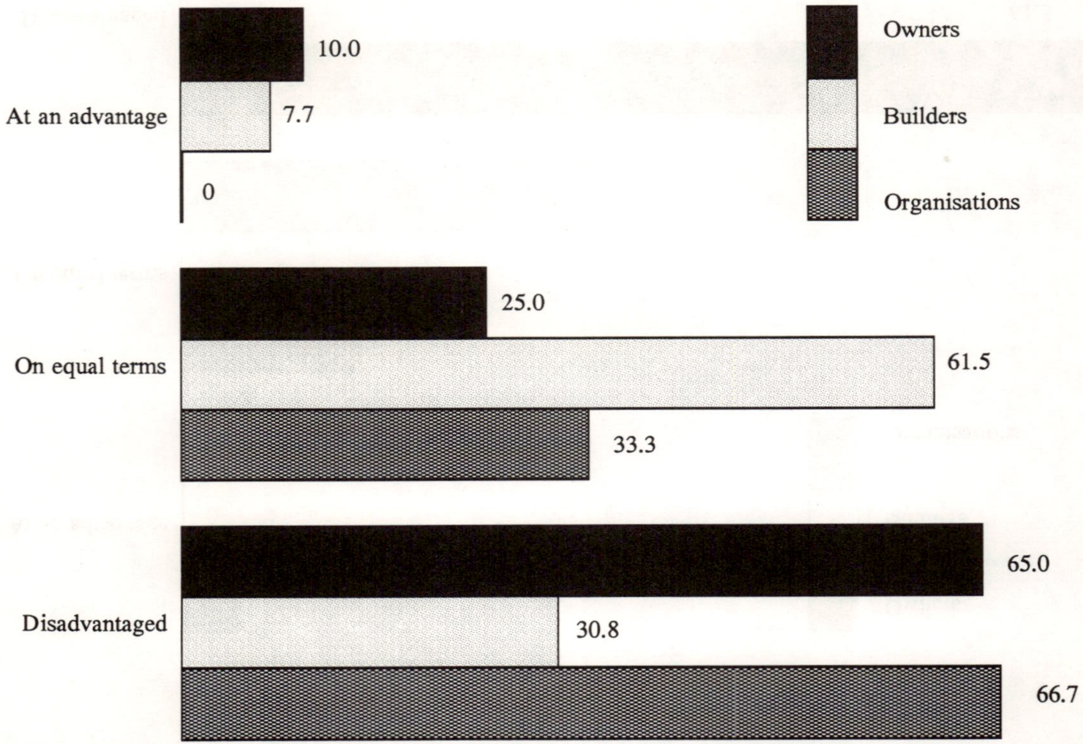

Owners
Builders
Organisations

At an advantage
10.0
7.7
0

On equal terms
25.0
61.5
33.3

Disadvantaged
65.0
30.8
66.7

Figure 5
Category of respondent – Netherlands

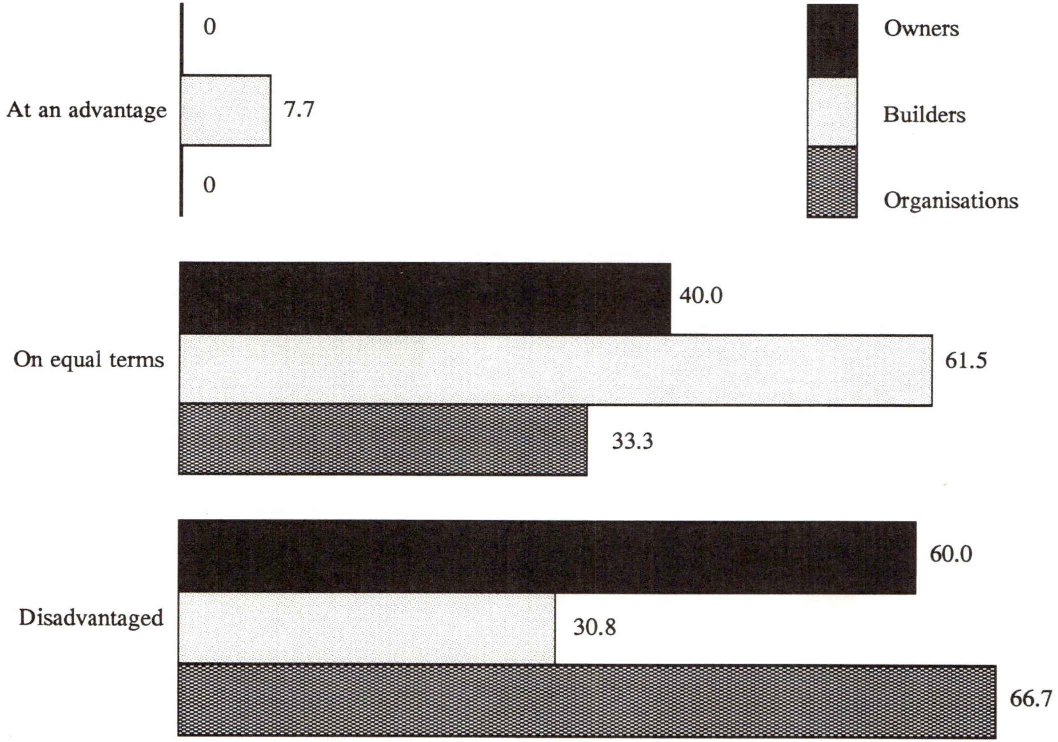

Owners
Builders
Organisations

At an advantage
0
7.7
0

On equal terms
40.0
61.5
33.3

Disadvantaged
60.0
30.8
66.7

Figure 6
Category of respondent – Germany

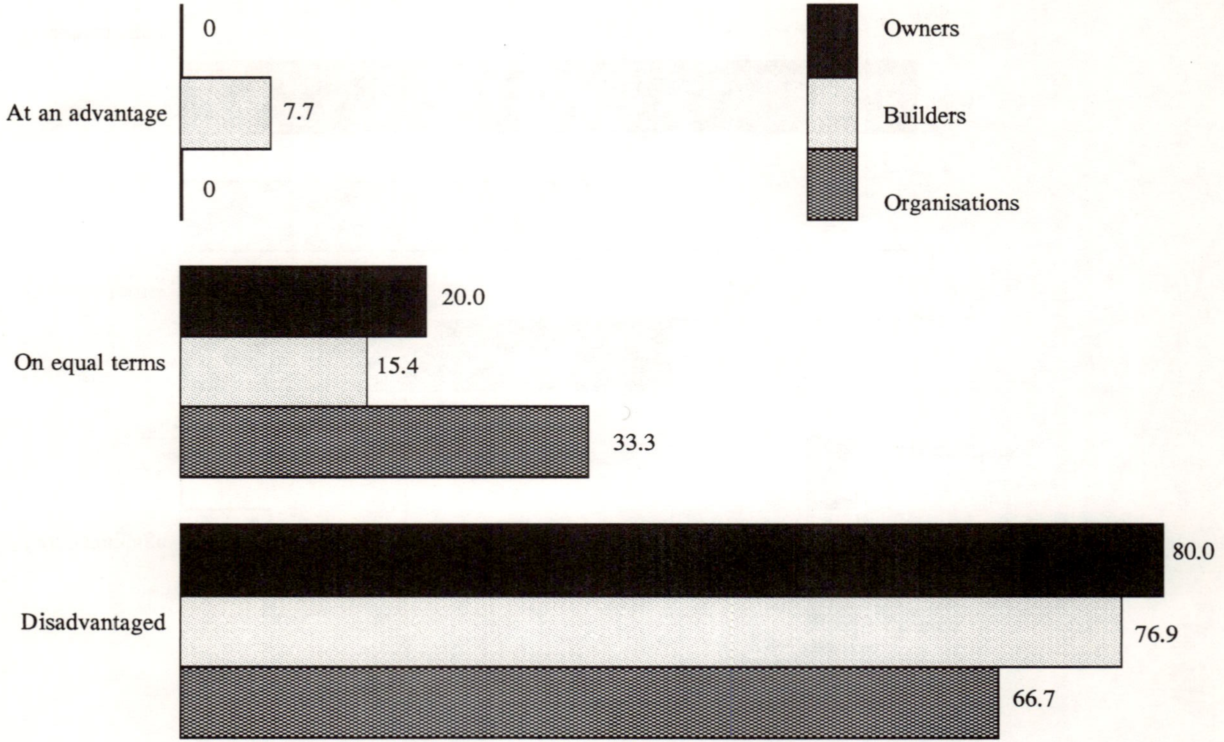

Legend:
- Owners
- Builders
- Organisations

At an advantage
- Owners: 0
- Builders: 7.7
- Organisations: 0

On equal terms
- Owners: 20.0
- Builders: 15.4
- Organisations: 33.3

Disadvantaged
- Owners: 80.0
- Builders: 76.9
- Organisations: 66.7

Whilst 45 per cent thought that subsidies should be granted to both coastal and 'deep sea' shipping, only 27 per cent felt that British companies operating under foreign flags should receive any form of subsidy.

Of these supporting subsidies to shipbuilding, 43 per cent felt that they should exist to protect local and subcontracted employment, 57 per cent to maintain capacity for strategic reasons and 48 per cent felt they should be administered for key sectors in industrial development strategy. That only 45 per cent of those in favour of shipping subsidies and 43 per cent in favour of building subsidies disagreed with the statement that 'they destroy commercial freedom' is strong evidence that operators know the disadvantages of subsidies but are prepared to accept them. Only 21 per cent believes 'they increase efficiency and competitiveness'. Overall 43 per cent of all respondents said they preferred subsidies to other forms of intervention such as trade barriers whilst 33 per cent did not.

But what form should these subsidies take? Figures 7 to 13 show respondents' opinions of how eleven types of subsidy satisfy their objectives. On the shipping side it was generally felt that of the direct subsidies, a construction subsidy was the most suitable and of the indirect possibilities investment allowances/grants and tax benefits were most appropriate. This was especially true of the latter which had the most support as an attempt to satisfy the aims stated on question six. On the shipbuilding side investment allowances/grants were seen as the most suitable indirect source of fulfilling the aims of question eight. On the direct side the strongest support was for construction subsidies.

In terms of legislation currently in existence there was significant support (seventy nine per cent) for a return to pre 1984 arrangements where shipowners were allowed to offset 100 per cent of a ship's value against profits for the first year of use and even more substantial desire (eighty three per cent) to see owners being allowed to retain profits in a tax free reserve against future investment in ships.

There was general agreement on the other fiscal incentives proposed by NUMAST and the GCBS. Fifty seven per cent of respondents said the government should give more favourable rates of seafarers income tax and fifty five per cent felt employers national insurance contributions should be reduced.

Forty eight per cent of respondents were satisfied with the UK corporation tax rates; thirty eight per cent were dissatisfied. There was a disappointing response to the question on agreement with the OECD understanding on ship export credits, 33 per cent didn't answer at all, presumably through lack of knowledge, whilst of those who did answer, 45 per cent were in agreement and 21 per cent in opposition.

Conclusions

Subsidies can be found in a number of forms and names depending upon the country of origin yet all have the same motive. Without governmental assistance the aided industries would not be as economically viable and in some cases would struggle to survive. This has significant implications at various levels, primarily national security. Certainly those companies operating in United Kingdom maritime industries believe so - the questionnaire results highlighted the development/protection of fleets and ensuring national security as the prime reasons for administering subsidies to the UK shipping and shipbuilding industries.

Britain's role as a traditional maritime nation and its historical power have eroded

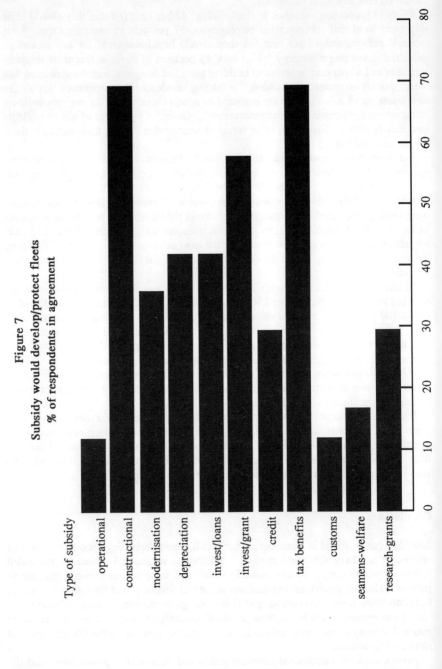

Figure 7
Subsidy would develop/protect fleets
% of respondents in agreement

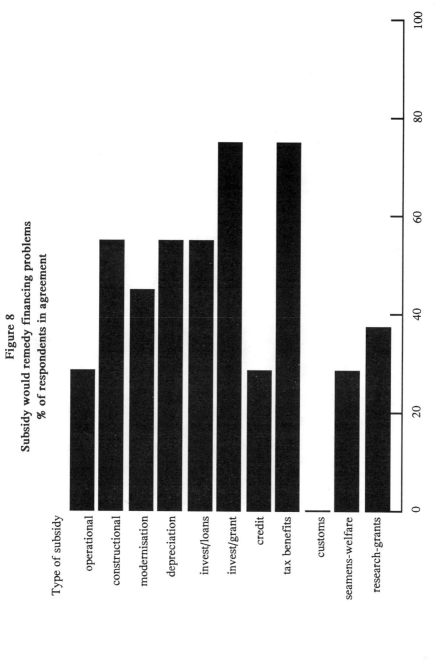

Figure 8
Subsidy would remedy financing problems
% of respondents in agreement

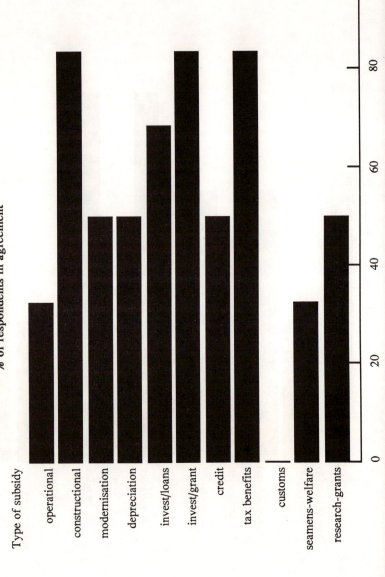

Figure 9

Subsidy would compensate social services

% of respondents in agreement

74

Figure 10
Subsidy would ensure national security
% of respondents in agreement

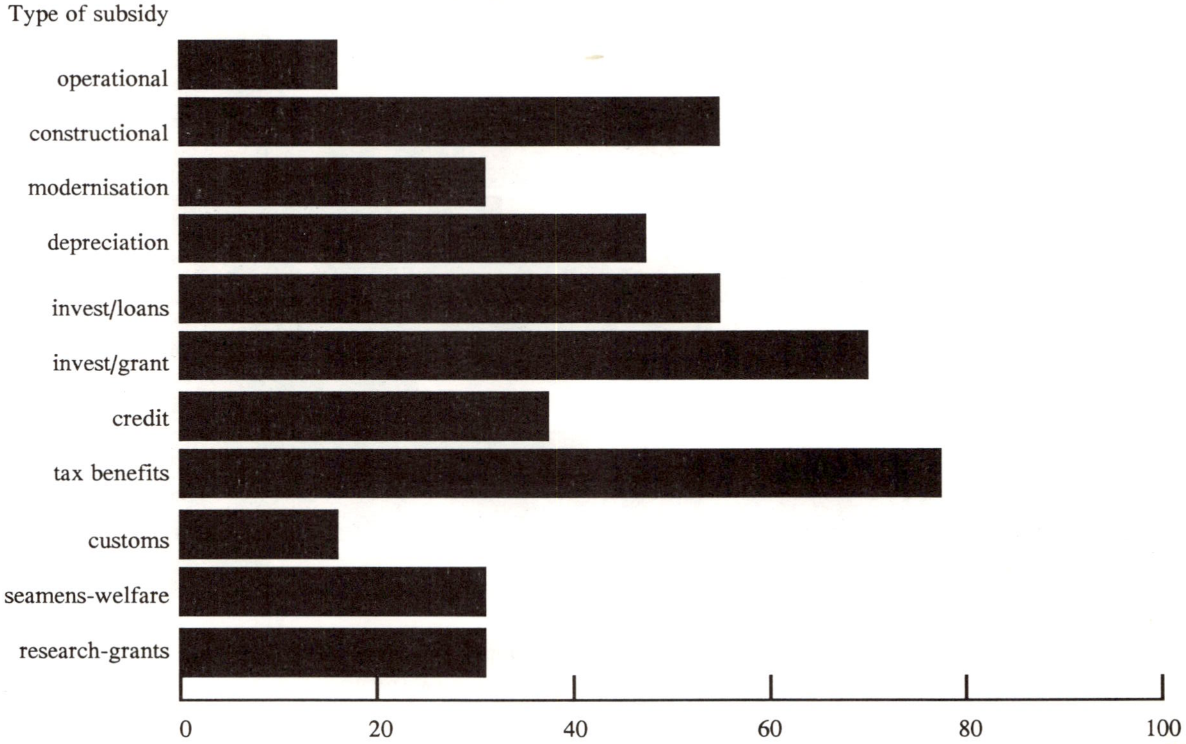

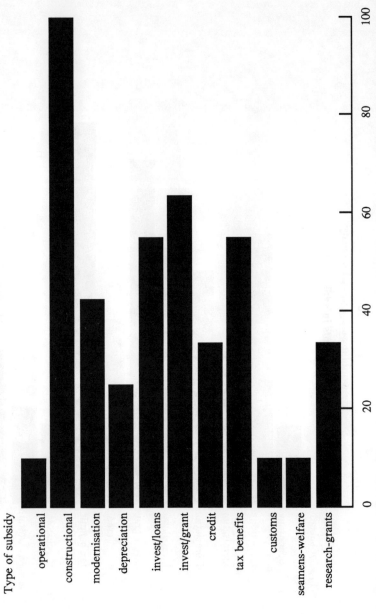

Figure 11
Subsidy would protect employment
% of respondents in agreement

Figure 12
Subsidy would maintain capacity
% of respondents in agreement

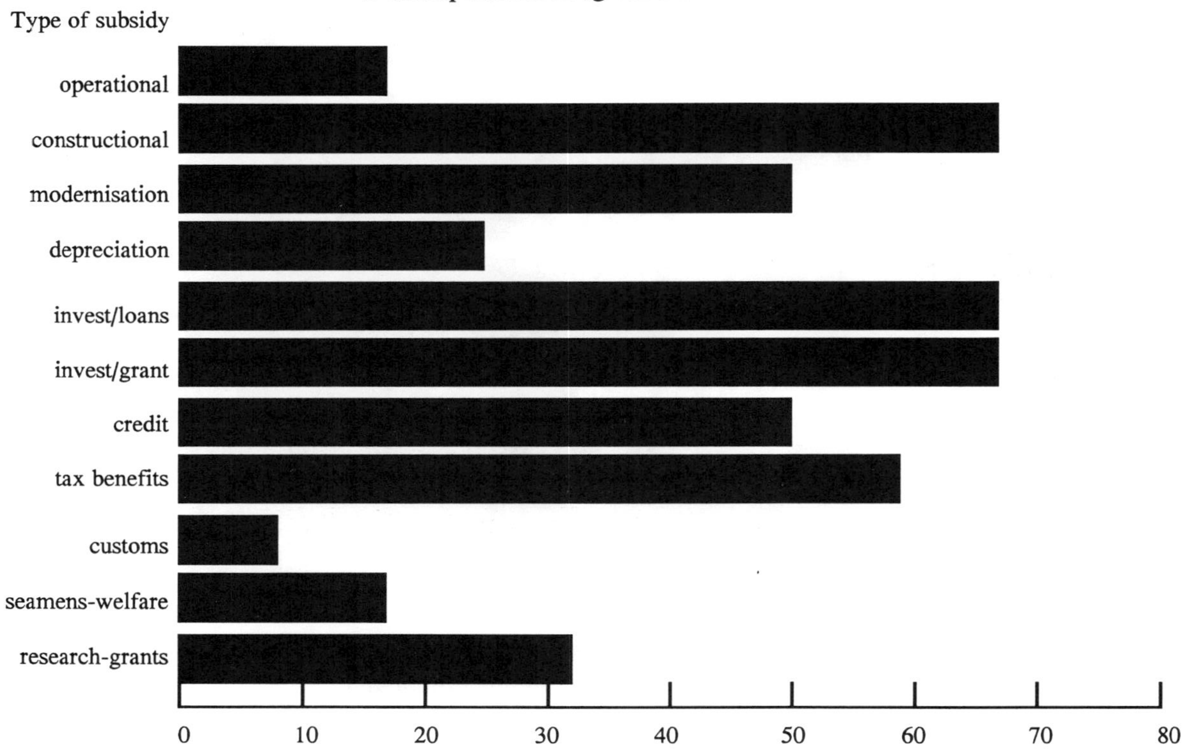

Type of subsidy

operational
constructional
modernisation
depreciation
invest/loans
invest/grant
credit
tax benefits
customs
seamens-welfare
research-grants

0   10   20   30   40   50   60   70   80

Figure 13
Subsidies given to key sectors
% of respondents in agreement

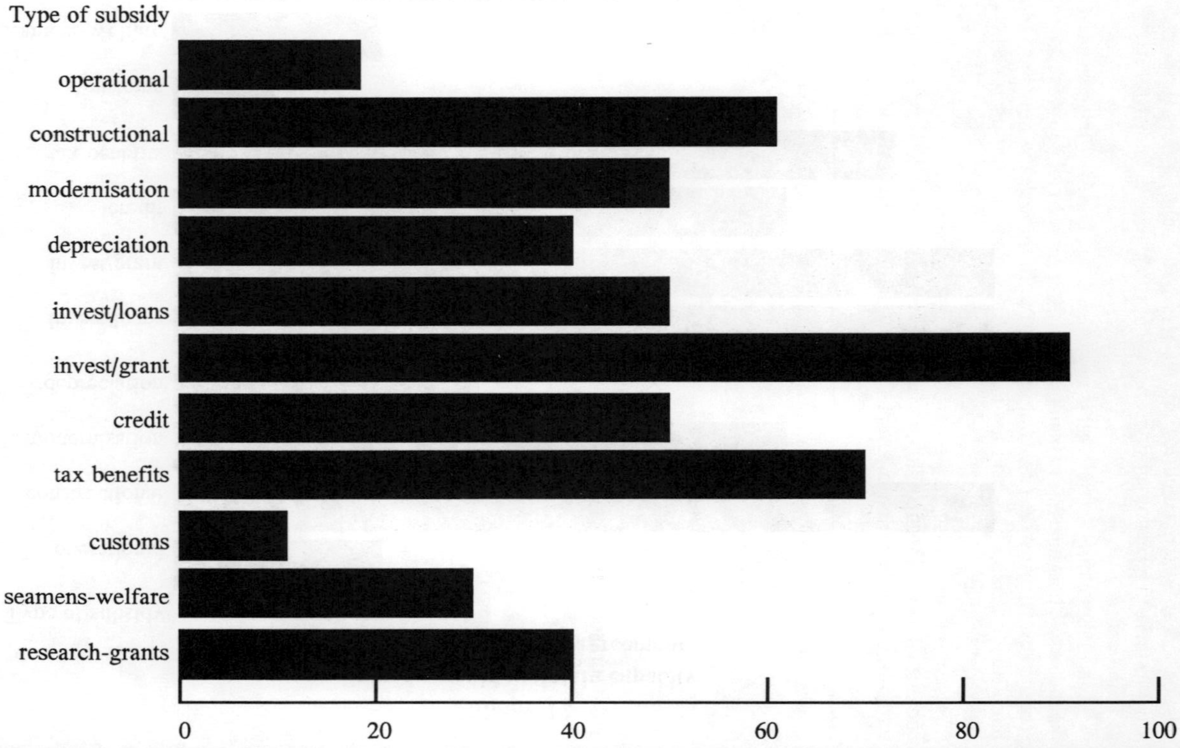

steadily since the second world war as both industries have struggled to be cost competitive. The respondents felt dissatisfied with their operating conditions compared to the four other countries in the survey who themselves are relatively subsidy free in relation to Far Eastern countries. Of the surveyed countries only Germany competes on a world scale in terms of subsidies but even its state aid is under threat due to the costs of reunification.

In the shipbuilding sector what is needed is a much greater understanding that it is in the industry's best interests to maintain contract prices on an upwards path towards more realistic levels. Any deviations in the short term through the heavy use of subsidies is likely to destabilize the industry to the extent that its long term recovery could be seriously delayed.

Moreover it is also naive to believe that subsidies which have become deeply entrenched in world shipbuilding can be completely removed over the short to medium term. Rather it is better to accept their continuing existence while working towards a common international understanding on the definition of subsidies and greater transparency in their application as part of the long term effort to reduce their relative significance in terms of competitive pricing within the market place. To this extent the EC directives of recent years have worked well although there is a growing impatience in the UK (not helped by the recessionary economy) to 'level the playing field' with other nations.

This is particularly true in the shipping sector where there is less clarity and negotiation of subsidies; UK operators have stated that they don't want to be 'propped up' but rather given the chance to compete with flags of convenience. They feel the tax and insurance changes highlighted earlier would allow them to prove that the British flag and seafarers are the safest and most efficient afloat.

The joint government/GCBS working party concluded that British shipping was a 'vital national asset' yet to quote one survey respondent 'This appears to be a low priority for both Tory and Labour governments despite the experience of the Falklands and the present Gulf crisis.'

References

Books

Ademuni - Odeke (1984), Protectionism and the future of international shipping, (Martinus Nijhoff).
Beth, H.L. Hader, A. Kapper, R. (1984) 25 Years of World Shipping, Fairplay Publications.
Branch, A.E. (1989), Elements of Shipping, Chapman & Hall.
British Maritime Charitable Foundation (1988), The Merchant Fleet and Britain's Economy,
British Overseas Trade Board (1989)(#), Belgium - A Profile.
British Overseas Trade Board (1989), France - A Profile.
Cafruny, A.W. (1987), Ruling the Waves, University of California Press.
Chrzanowski, I. (1985), An Introduction to Shipping Economics, Fairplay Publications.
Department of Trade & Industry (1972), British Shipbuilding, HMSO.
Department of Transport/GCBS (1990), British Shipping: Challenges and Opportunities, HMSO.

Drewry Shipping Consultants Ltd (1985), Prospects for World Shipbuilding : Forecast Output to 1994.

Eversheim, F. (1958), Effects of Shipping Subsidization, BREMEN: Institute for Shipping Research.

Fairplay (1990), Fairplay World Shipping Directory 1990-1991, Fairplay Information Systems Ltd.

Farthing, B., International Shipping, Lloyds of London Press Ltd.

Farthing, R.C. (1979), Shipping and Shipbuilding subsidies. I. Ryden C. von Schirach - SZMIGIEL (eds.), Shipping and Ships for the 1990s, Economic Research Institute.

Frankel, E.G. (1987), The World Shipping Industry, Croom Helm.

General Council of British Shipping (1981), British Shipping Statistics.

Gereral Council of British Shipping (1989), A Level Playing Field for Merchant Shipping.

General Council of British Shipping (1991), Joint Government/Industry Working Party on British Shipping - Further submission by GCBS on fiscal issues.

Hogwood, B.W. (1979), Governments and Shipbuilding - The politics of industrial change, Saxon House.

House of Commons Transport Committee (1987-88), First Report on the Decline in the UK Registered Merchant Fleet, vol. 3, HMSO.

MAN - B & W Diesel (1982), Financing and Subsidizing the Marine Industries.

National Union of Marine Aviation and Shipping Transport Officers (1991a), British Shipping - Not a Sunset Industry - Submission for the 1991 Budget.

National Union of Marine Aviation and Shipping Transport Officers (1991b), Personal Correspondence.

Organization for Economic Cooperation and Development (1963), Code of liberalization of current invisible operations.

Seatrade (1978), EEC Shipping 1978, Seatrade Publications.

United States Department of Commerce (1977), The Maritime Aids of the Six Major Maritime Nations.

Journals

'Belgian Marine Industry', Fairplay, 8 March 1979, pp. 37-41.

'Progress towards a common transport policy - maritime transport', Bulletin of the European Communities, supplement May 1985.

'Shipbuilding in Holland, France and Belgium', Shipping World and Shipbuilder, May 1987, pp. 161-163.

'Ready for Challenge with Substantial Order Cushion', Seatrade Business Review, May/June 1989, pp. 83-89.

'Need for a new maritime vision', Transport, April 1990, p.67.

Shipping Statistics and Economics, July 1990, No. 237.

'Shipping subsidies should go says Platou', Lloyds Shipping Manager, July 1990, pp. 61-61.

'West Germany cuts yard subsidies', Fairplay, 12 July 1990, p.5.

'Boelwerf Shipyard Returns from the Brink', Motor Ship, January 1991, pp. 44-47.

'Mixed reaction from Brussels subsidy meeting', Fairplay, 10 January 1991, pp. 25-26.

'Budget is vital for UK fleet', Telegraph, March 1991, p.1.

'Orders slump', Telegraph, April 1991, p.19.

Lloyds List

'Shipyards Braced for Day of Truth', 22 January 1991, p.3.
'UK Lowers Building Subsidies', 6 February 1991, p.1.
'German Direct Aid to Owners Halted', 9 February 1991, p.3.
'Budget Change Call for Seamen', 11 February 1991, p.2.
'Severe Cuts are Forecast at East German Yards', 11 February 1991, p.2.
'French Yard Set for £1.3 billion Deal', 12 February 1990, p.1.
'French Yard Wins Petronas Contract', 13 February 1991, p.1.
'Keep the Red Flag Flying', 19 February 1991, p.4.

Lloyds Shipping Economist

'Perspectives', June 1986, p.34.
'Taxing Problems Facing BES Shipping Ventures', April 1989, p.10.
'Tricolour Aid in the 1990s', October 1989, p.2.
'Twelve Press on Towards Unity', February 1990, pp. 6-8.
'Open for Business or Fortress Europe?', February 1990, pp. 12-13.
'EC Slashes Subsidy Ceiling', January 1991, p.3.

4 EUROS: The European Community ship register

Brian Smith

Introduction

The legal regime of the ship

It is a rule of international law that a ship cannot conveniently trade or enjoy the benefits of nationality without being registered under the law of a state - entitling the ship to fly the flag of that state (its 'flag state'). Every state, coastal or landlocked, has the right to sail ships flying its flag on the high seas. The ship's flag gives it its nationality.

A flag state has jurisdiction over its ships wheresoever the ships may be (subject always to any port state and coastal state jurisdiction).

> Perhaps the most venerable and universal rule of maritime law…is that which gives cardinal importance to the law of the flag. Each state under international law may determine for itself the conditions on which it will grant nationality to a merchant ship, thereby accepting responsibility for it and acquiring authority over it. (Lauritzen v Larsen (1953) US571 at 584).

Registration gives nationality to a ship, it provides a means of identifying a ship and her owners (a ship's 'passport' is its Certificate of Registry), it evinces title to a ship, and it aids a mortgage. UK Registration for instance, dates from the Navigation Act, 1660, intending to reserve British trade for British vessels. Any state having a separate system of municipal law may issue regulations governing the registration of ships under its flag. This was recognized by the 1958 Geneva Convention on the High Seas which provides, in Article 5.1, that

> Each state shall fix the conditions for the grant of its nationality to ships, for the registration of ships in its territory, and for the right to fly its flag. Ships have the

nationality of the state whose flag they are entitled to fly. There must exist a genuine link between the state and the ship; in particular the state must effectively exercise its jurisdiction and control in administrative, technical and social matters over ships flying its flag.

(This article is echoed in the 1982 United Nations Convention on the Law of the Sea, and in the 1986 United Nations Convention on Conditions for Registration of Ships.)

The 1958 convention leaves open the question as to what the conditions for registration of ships should be - 'a genuine link' must exist and the flag state must effectively exercise jurisdiction and 'administrative, technical and social' control over its ships; but the strength of the 'link' and the degree of 'control; are presently left to be determined by each individual state.

For example, in the UK the 1988 Merchant Shipping Act allows a ship to be entered on the register where a minority interest - less than or equal to 32 out of 64 shares (a British ship is notionally divided into 64 shares) - in the ship is owned by unqualified persons; prior to the 1988 Act all the shares in a British ship had to be owned by qualified persons.

The Act further provides that where the majority interest owner is not resident in the United Kingdom a 'representative person' must be appointed within the UK (Merchant Shipping Act, 1988, Section 4). There are no requirements as to the nationality of directors but the master and chief officer must be British.

In Greece fifty per cent of the shareholders in the owning company must be Greek nationals while the master and seventy per cent of the crew must be Greek.

In the USA the majority of directors must be USA nationals and the ship must be built in the USA; there is no equity requirement regarding nationals but 100 per cent of officers and seventy five per cent of crew must be USA nationals.

Some states therefore adhere strictly to the 'genuine link' principle - admitting to their registers only those ships which are owned and controlled by resident nationals (individuals, corporations or partnerships) of the flag state, and manned (wholly or in part) by its nationals (with some states admitting only ships built in its shipyards - eg the USA).

Other states adopt a wholly relaxed attitude to the genuine link principle; to them the mere fact of registration is a sufficient genuine link - their registries are 'open' to ships beneficially owned and controlled from outside the flag state.

Flags of convenience/open registry

Not all registries or flags are entirely 'convenient' therefore for all shipowners; consequently many states allow, indeed encourage, registration of foreign owned ships, this being a source of revenue. There are also significant advantages which attract the shipowners to the flags of convenience concept; taxes and crew costs are lower and labour laws, safety requirements, construction rules and ship inspections are possibly less stringent since many flag of convenience states exercise little or no effective administrative control over their ships. These substantially lower costs make the ship more competitive in the international freight market.

The overriding reasons why owners opt for 'open registry' are summarized below:

(i) Operating flexibility   Ships in 'open registry' can be operated with minimum

constraints. There are no restrictions on where the ship must be built or repaired and no tax is imposed on repairs made outside the country of registry as would be the case, for example, if it were a US registered ship. The shipowner, as well as not being required to be a citizen of the country of registry, is also not subject to extensive government trade and financial reporting requirements. Vessels are not restricted as to ports they may enter, or customers that may be served (a vessel may trade virtually anywhere in the world without political restrictions imposed by the flag state). In America, for instance, vessels are prohibited by law to enter certain ports.

The country of registry has neither the power nor the administrative machinery effectively to impose any government or international regulations; nor have the country the wish or the power to control the companies themselves. This operating freedom is a great incentive then for the shipowner.

(ii) Ability to choose optimum manning source   This means that under 'open registry' shipowners can choose their personnel from a worldwide manpower pool. The owner can select the most cost effective manning source, which is probably where government or union imposed work rules are minimal or non existent; crews from developing countries can be employed at local rates of pay.

(iii) Freedom from taxation   Apart from registration and annual fees, open registry countries generally impose no tax on shipowners' income. A registry fee and annual fee, based on tonnage, are normally the only charges made. Today though, taxation is almost a secondary reason, reduced manning costs being the main one. Indeed many countries exempt their national flagged fleets from taxes to try and encourage their shipping to stay in the country.

(iv) Financing requirement   Sometimes shipowners do not choose to place their vessels in 'open registry' but are forced to by circumstances. Often in developing countries a shipowner must place his vessel in an open registry as a condition of obtaining finance. This is because not all countries have an Admiralty code which establishes lien enforcement conditions acceptable to lenders. It is widely accepted that registration in Liberia or Panama assures payment is enforceable in the courts.

(v) Operating and safety standards   It has been reported that operating and safety standards are lower and not enforced in 'open registries' where ships sometimes never even touch their home ports. As far as operating standards are concerned, this appears to be mainly unfounded as ships represent massive investment and it would not be worthwhile to let them deteriorate. Safety standards of open registry ships have tended to produce unsatisfactory casualty records, but some flag of convenience states have taken action to correct this shortcoming.

(vi) Political uncertainties   Shipowners in countries with potential unrest may choose open registry as neutral territory.

(vii) Neutral flag   In circumstances requiring low profile trading, a shipowner, often with government encouragement, places his ship in 'open registry'. Israeli and South African shipowners have used 'open registry' for this purpose.

'Open registries' have a history dating back many centuries, almost from the time goods were transported by sea. During the sixteenth and seventeenth centuries English shipowners placed vessels in Spanish or French registry to avoid trading and fishing restrictions and sailing vessels in the eighteenth century, particularly in the Mediterranean trades, switched flag depending on their trade and which state offered the best protection. However, 'open registry' really began to develop in the 1920s when the US and Panama (the forerunner of the 'open registry' concept) made a treaty exempting shipping profits from taxes. The Panamanian flag also enabled American oil companies to supply Britain despite American neutrality in the early years of the second world war and also let them use British seamen instead of Americans on ships under the Panamanian flag.

Liberia emerged as a flag of convenience in 1950 with the drafting of the Liberian maritime law. This established a system for recording mortgages acceptable for lending institutions. Shipowners liked the system and Liberia quickly built up a much larger fleet than Panama. Today there are many open registries; Liberia, Panama, Cyprus, Bahamas, Hong Kong and Singapore are the main ones but there are many more smaller countries as well.

The following table comprehensively illustrates the growing influence and impact of flags of convenience. To be noted against this is the dramatic decline in the EEC fleet; this current 'flagging out' by European shipowners is indicative that their national flags are not entirely acceptable.

Table 1
Merchant fleets as a percentage of total world tonnage 1988

Fleet	1988	1975
Flags of convenience	35.0	25.9
Rest of the world	24.3	9.2
Other OECD	18.4	28.4
EEC	15.4	30.8
COMECON	6.9	5.5

New systems of registration

In recent years developed countries have given birth to new systems of ship registration in order to deter shipowners from flagging out to flag of convenience countries. Such a system may be established with the developed country itself (via an 'international' register) or in a country's dependent territory (via an offshore register). These registries afford the crew the costs and taxation advantages of the open registries while having almost the same status as their 'parent' registers.

For example, a significant development in the mid 1980s onwards was the tendency for some UK shipowners to 'flag out' their fleets into the independent territory category of the Isle of Man - this registration mirrors the British system and, in addition to the tax haven status of the island, seafarers can be employed without payment of employer's UK National Insurance and pension contributions that would be payable under the UK rules and crewing agreements. A number of UK and Danish shipowners for example, have transferred to the Isle of Man and their crews offered new employment.

A more recent development is the emergence of offshore registries which run in tandem with the mainland European registries from which they derive. The Norwegian International Ship Registry (NIS) is an example which was introduced by the Norwegian Government in 1987. It is open to both Norwegian and foreign shipowners and permits them to employ foreign crews other than masters. Favourable tax treatment is given to foreign crews and, with salaries below a certain limit, the crews are exempt altogether from Norwegian taxes. Certification and safety requirements are identical to those of the main register so that safety standards should not be prejudiced. By 1988, 4.9 million GRT involving 155 ships had registered on the NIS register.

Bareboat charter

Parallel with the development of international and offshore registries has been the introduction of the bareboat charter dual registers. The owner of a ship, registered under an established and well respected 'flag' , forms a company in a flag of convenience country, bareboat charters his ship to the newly formed company and registers the ship under the flag of the bareboat charterer's state.

Under the dual registry system the ship's original registration is not cancelled; the ship remains entered on the original register whilst flying a flag of convenience. (The laws of both the original flag state and the flag of convenience state must allow such a transaction.) The bareboat company may operate the ship or it may transfer the management of the ship back to her owner.

Such a system of registry affords a shipowner the best of both worlds - the operation of the ship is subject to the flag of convenience state's jurisdiction, whilst the ship's mortgage remains under the law of the original flag state.

Open registry is therefore a major problem for the European Community flags, as well as to other maritime nations. Opponents of open registry flags argue that the employment of third world crews at lower than European rates of pay represents exploitation of the individuals concerned. They argue therefore that vessels should be flagged in the state of beneficial ownership, employing crews of the same nationality. Shipping though, is a very expensive business and extremely competitive, therefore owners want to make the largest savings possible. Shipping companies tend to pay for their new ships out of past profits, and it is those companies operating under the flags of countries of low taxation, cheaper manning costs and cheaper running costs that have been able to expand their fleets. Conversely the owners of other fleets, especially those in the EEC, whose costs are much higher, have been unable to expand to take advantage of increased demand. The European Community hopes that, through its proposed European flag registry, EUROS, it can challenge the rise in influence and impact of flags of convenience.

The EC shipping policy

The fathers of the Treaty of Rome (signed 25 March 1957 forming the European Community) said that the objectives of the Treaty shall be pursued in the transport sector by a common policy. The objectives of the Treaty are, in very general terms, describing harmonious development of the economy, promotion of better living and working conditions in Europe, etc. In this respect the general rules of the Treaty are concerned with the establishment of the basic freedoms for undertakings in the common market, right of establishment, free movement of services, etc., and rules concerning the functioning of the common market, mainly the competition rules and the prohibition of state aids. One can see therefore, that the basic policy of the community is based on market economy principles. The question is how these basic considerations fit into the shipping sector. We must first look at the basic structure of this sector before defining the objectives in more detail.

Historical and factual background

Firstly one must consider that the community depends for its foreign trade almost entirely on reliable and efficient shipping services. Historically, sea borne trade and merchant fleets have been of great importance in the development of Europe's maritime nations. The community is the biggest trading bloc in the world and about ninety per cent of its foreign trade is carried by sea.

The shipping industry also has an important role in the community's internal trade where it carries about one third of the 750 million tonnes of goods exchanged each year between the member states.

The participation of European flags in the community's foreign trade is around 70 per cent of internal trade and 40 per cent of external trade. In addition, community shipowners earn part of their income by cross trading between third countries. The community is basically therefore a maritime nation. Its interest lies in free trading on an open worldwide shipping market.

Here lies the source of some difficulties. The first difficulty is the oversupply of ships on the world market. In recent years European domination of world seaborne trade and shipping tonnage has been challenged by the growth of 'open registry' countries, and of third world countries, and the EEC maritime policy also faces problems from the sevenfold increase in the COMECON container fleet, which is in direct competition with the EEC container fleet. World seaborne trade peaked in 1979, followed by a steady decline both in tonnes and in the more significant tonne miles, which represents the actual demand for shipping. From 1979 to 1984, the tonne miles performance of the world fleet dropped by twenty five per cent. The shipping industry helped itself with lay up schemes and scrapping programmes. However, today there remains an excess tonnage in world shipping estimated at about twenty per cent. This excess capacity leads to big pressure on the level of freight rates, and to protectionist measures on the part of some developing countries struggling to set up their own fleet.

Added to this already difficult situation, community shipowners have to cope with the fact that Europe is a high cost environment for their business and their competitive conditions are thus unfavourable. This has led to an impressive decline of the community fleet in the sense of ships registered under the flag of one of the member states. Whereas ten years ago about one third of world tonnage was registered in the community, in 1987 it was only slightly more than sixteen per cent. This has naturally led also to a big decrease in employment of community seafarers under European flags.

EC shipping policy up to 1985

The development of a European shipping policy is relatively recent bearing in mind the Treaty of Rome was signed back in 1957 and originally excluded any form of maritime policy. Not until the UK joined the community (in 1973) did the EC agree that shipping should be included in the policy. Britain made representations about the lack of such a policy; the Council of Ministers were taken to court and it was decided that seafarers did indeed require a policy, formulated in the beginning with a submission to council in 1976 of a communication on shipping matters and relationships with third countries.

Briefly, the areas covered were as follows:

(i) Social areas Articles 48-51 EEC and deriving secondary law, i.e. of the acquis communantaire in this area of shipping can be subsumed into the following:

- Free movement of community seafarers among member states' flagged vessels.
- Employment on board these vessels on the same level as nationals of the flag state.
- Community preference regarding seafarers of third states.
- Measures on pensions and other social security benefits.

The Hollesen study (1985) revealed significant differences between the fleets of the member countries concerning seafarers' pay and their working conditions.

(ii) Right to establishment Articles 52-58 of the Treaty of Rome on sea transport mean that national provisions restricting the right of establishment of shipping companies from a member state to a member state are inapplicable vis-a-vis nationals or companies; such infringements may be brought before national courts.

For now, with the exception of the UK and Ireland, national legislation reserves in varying degrees the right of registration of vessels to nationals or national companies.

(iii) Competition rules Controversy has arisen among the member states over a set of rules put forward by the Commission. The draft regulation, which is generally concerned with sea transport, propounds the conditions under which liner conferences may be granted exemption.

(iv) Eastern Bloc Action was initiated by a communication of the Commission to the council (June 1976) requesting counter measures to be taken against the Eastern Bloc. Along with this the Seefeld Report to the European parliament (March 1977) recommended the need for appropriate measures.

The problem was that the Eastern Bloc wanted hard currency and to obtain it they undercut the West - made possible because their vessels could operate with no commercial criteria. COMECON countries accumulated hard currencies to pay for imports of Western commodities and technology and EC shipping suffered considerably.

Though the community could do little, they did set up a monitoring system on abuse of the freedom of the seas.

(v) Safety of navigation and pollution prevention at sea In response to a number of tanker accidents causing pollution in community waters, action was taken by the community in the form of several acts.

Two directives concerning pilotage in the North Sea and the English Channel and the minimum requirements for certain tankers entering or leaving EC ports were produced.

Two recommendations urged the member states to ratify the 1978 Convention of IMCO on standards of training, certification and watchkeeping of seafarers, the 1974 IMCO Safety of Life at Sea Convention (SOLAS), the 1973 IMCO Prevention of Maritime Pollution Convention (MARPOL) and their 1978 Protocols as well as the International Labour Organization Convention No 147 on minimum safety standards of vessels.

(vi) Measures relating to the 1979 UNCTAD liner code It was agreed that the Liner Conference Code, Regulation 954/79, of 15 May 1979, with its famous 40-40-20 formula (whereby 40 per cent of sea transport is carried by liner vessels of the exporter country, 40 per cent by liners of the importer country and 20 per cent by third flag carriers) would be ratified according to the following reservations:

a) the code will apply to trade between developing and developed countries;
b) it will not apply in trades between EC countries and on a reciprocal basis between EC and OECD countries;
c) the share allocated under the Code to the EC lines will be redistributed among them on the basis of commercial criteria.

(vii) Shipbuilding The shipbuilding industry was affected severely by the prolonged slump in freight markets; between 1976 and 1979 according to figures produced by Lloyds, vessel completions by community shipyards fell by forty two per cent whilst the corresponding decrease worldwide was thirty seven per cent. The difference in percentages was due to competitive disadvantages that the community fleet faced, among them high operating costs.

The community has so far issued five Directives on harmonizing subsidy/aid to shipbuilding as well as entering into negotiations with Far Eastern countries, Japan for instance, to try and reduce shipbuilding overcapacity.

Post 1985

On 16 December 1986 the maritime package was agreed by the European Community ministers and, together with measures already adopted since 1977, formed the basis of a community policy in the maritime field.

The package included four regulations:

- Council Regulation (EEC) No. 4055/86 of 22 December 1986, applying the principle of freedom to provide services to maritime transport between member states and third countries.
- Council Regulation (EEC) No. 4057/86 of 22 December 1986, on unfair pricing practices in maritime transport.
- Council Regulation (EEC) No. 4056/86 of 22 December 1986, laying down detailed rules for application of Articles 85 and 86 of the Treaty to maritime transport.
- Council Regulation (EEC) No. 4058/86 of 22 December 1986, concerning coordinated action to safeguard free access to cargoes in ocean trades.

The four regulations

No. 4055/86. Freedom to provide services This regulation introduced the principle of freedom to provide services (embodying the principle of non discrimination) to intra community trade; it distinguished between existing arrangements and future agreements. It applies to nationals and shipping companies of member states established in the community and its purpose is to prevent any member state from discriminating in favour of its own shipping companies to the disadvantage of shipping companies in another member state.

The regulation applies to both intra community traffic and to traffic between member states and third countries, but not to the domestic trade of a member state, i.e. it does not apply to cabotage.

No. 4056/86. Competition rules This regulation aims at the effective application of the Treaty competition rules (Articles 85 and 86) to shipping and applies to all international shipping services to and from one or more community ports, other than tramp services. It exempts liner cargo conferences en bloc from the Treaty's provisions on restrictive practices, subject to certain conditions and obligations; for example, users must be consulted on rates, conditions and quality of services. The intention is to provide a balance between the interests of conferences and those of shippers.

This regulation differentiates between conferences operating in open trades (where non conference competition is possible) and those operating in closed trades (where non conference competition is ruled out) and in effect sets a more relaxed regime for the open than for the closed trades.

No. 4057/86. Unfair pricing practices This regulation (applying to liner trades) empowered the Commission to impose a compensatory duty (fine) on non EEC shipowners if the following conditions exist and are cumulatively present:

i)   evidence of unfair pricing practices (defined as undercutting community shipping services where this is made possible by the fact that non EEC shipowners enjoy non commercial advantages, such as subsidy, preferential legislation, etc.);

ii) evidence of them causing injury to EEC shipping lines;

iii) evidence that the interests of the community would benefit by the community intervening and the company concerned being fined.

Any natural or legal person or association feeling injured of threatened by unfair pricing practices can lodge a complaint on behalf of the community shipping industry, giving evidence of such practices.

Compensatory duties may be imposed if evidence is found to justify the complaint but regulations must take account of external trade and shipping policy considerations (in case one 'upsets' another country).

No. 4058/86. Coordinated action This regulation provides for coordinated community action designed to tackle third party governments (third countries) - people outside the community - who restrict access of EEC shipping companies to ocean trades and give preference to their own shipping lines; flag discriminations.

The Commission is allowed to enter premises, seize documents and possibly impose fines if discriminating evidence is found.

Although these four regulations focused in particular on the threat of community shipping from protectionist policies and practices of third countries, there was a clear need for further development of the community policy in order to maintain and develop an efficient and competitive community shipping industry.

It was 5 June 1989 before progress was made when the Commission presented to the Council of Ministers the proposals for stage 2 of the European Community Shipping Policy.

The Commission of the European Communities drew up a list of measures to improve the operating conditions of the community fleet and a report was published on 3 August 1989. The current state of the shipping industry and its relation to the community was detailed, the need for community action and the measures to be taken were all contained in the publication.

Changes in world and community shipping

The protracted oversupply of shipping services worldwide, and the consequent fall in freight rates, precipitated a serious decline of the community's merchant fleet. Over a prolonged period markets were characterized by freight rates that were so low that only those ships with the highest levels of productivity could compete effectively.

The increased competition had serious consequences for the community fleet, which contracted rapidly and this meant increased dependence on the services of third country operators, lost foreign exchange earnings, lost employment, lost influence in international trade and shipping negotiations and lost orders for community shipyards.

This decline can be more specifically detailed:

a) Reduced demand for world shipping services Cargo movements by sea in 1988, measured by tonne miles, were still nine per cent below the 1980 level, following a disastrous fall by twenty four per cent between 1980 and 1983. This drop represented not only a fall in the total volume of seaborne trade but, more significantly, a fall in the distances in which this trade was carried.

There were two reasons for this and they concerned the relationship between the level of economic activity and that of seaborne trade.

Firstly, the upturn which the world economy experienced during the last few years was not accompanied by an equivalent increase in seaborne cargo volumes.

Secondly, changes in trade patterns were leading seaborne transport to and from industrialized countries to grow more slowly than the expanding world economy.

b) Fleet developments and the decline of the community fleet After years of expansion, the community's shipping capacity contracted sharply in the 1980s.

Since 1980 the tonnage registered in the eleven maritime member states fell from 117 million gross tons to 59 million tons in 1988 - a decrease of about fifty per cent while the number of ships fell from 11,218 to 6,512. As a share of the world fleet, community registered tonnage in 1988 was 15.4 per cent compared with more than 29.7 per cent in 1980. This falling trend in EC registered ships continued in 1990 and it is still continuing.

To a large extent the reduction was the result of 'flagging out' by shipowners although the community owned fleet as a whole also significantly reduced. Each of the member states' fleets is smaller now than it was in 1980, with the exception of Belgium whose fleet continued to grow until 1986. The largest tonnage falls have been in the Greek and UK registered fleets, which together account for two thirds of the decline in the community registered fleet.

c) Relative ageing of the community fleet Apart from the case of the Federal Republic and Denmark, the reduction of older tonnage through flagging out as well as increased scrapping was not accompanied by a modernization of the community's fleet. The community registered fleet is now older than most of its competitors.

This ageing is reflected in the reduced level of investment in new ships meaning a reduced opportunity to benefit from developments in shipbuilding design and construction aimed at increasing operational efficiency and reducing running costs. The continuation of such a trend would contribute further to a loss of competitiveness in the community fleet.

d) Shrinkage in employment The contraction of the community fleet and the development of more technologically advanced ships with lower manning requirements led to reduced seagoing employment. The total number of seafarers employed in the community fell by about 138,000 or some forty five percent between 1980 and 1986 to barely 169,000. In 1980, the community registered fleet employed about 54,000 seafarers of nationalities other than that of the flag state out of a total of about 307,0000.

The competitive disadvantage of the community fleet

The acute competition and cuts in freight rates have led to the relatively much greater decline in the community fleet and placed it in a position of comparative disadvantage. In the past, community fleets have countered competition by maintaining a technological lead and providing a higher quality of service, but in recent years third country fleets have expanded with modern vessels to at least match technically the community and the cost disadvantages of operating under community flags have proved too great for many shipowners. Whilst world market conditions have now improved very significantly, the problem of comparative disadvantage remains.

In part there have been the growth of protectionist measures by third countries and unfair pricing practices which have now been combatted by the council regulations contained in the maritime package of December 1986.

To compete effectively, however, community shipping has to face the problem of loss of comparative advantage. Reducing crew costs have been the main reason why shipowners have 'flagged out'. Third country crews have been so much cheaper not only because basic wages have been lower but also because the seafarers taxes and social security contributions are lower or non existent. Tax treatment of shipping companies must also be taken into account in this connection; a company established in an open register country does not pay any corporate income tax.

Certain member states also require their shipowners to build their vessels in national shipyards, at prices higher than they would pay in the world market; in at least one country they have to pay an import duty when permitted to buy abroad. The resulting burdens on the price of the ship are quite heavy.

Measures taken by member states

Member states have responded in a variety of ways to tackle the increasing tendency of shipowners operating under their national registers to transfer their vessels to open registers outside the community. Measures have been introduced with the main aim of reducing operating costs.

In a number of member states, the use of existing offshore registers has been greatly expanded, or new offshore or 'international' registers have been established. These registers enable member states to compete with lower costs by easing the conditions under which vessels are operated; through lower registration costs, little or no taxation and the employment of non community seafarers on non community wages and conditions.

It is clear then from this summary of the current state of the community shipping fleet that there are many problems. To quote the Commission:-

Only a combination of concerted measures, taken at community and national level with the necessary participation and cooperation of shipowners and seafarers can have the required positive impact on the operating conditions of community shipping.

Sufficient incentive must be provided so that community shipowners will register their ships within the community and will man those ships, to the highest possible proportion, with community seafarers. This will happen if the operating conditions of the community fleet improve the fleet's competitive position in the world market.

Basic criteria for establishing community shipping action

The Commission concluded that a very effective means of assisting the community fleet would be the establishment of a community register, EUROS, which would run in parallel to existing national registers. This is discussed later. Below are briefly summarized the further measures proposed by the Commission to improve the competitive position of the community fleet:

a) Manning and research Manning costs are the main reason behind the competitive disadvantage of the community regarding its competitors of third countries. A research fund should be set up to improve technical efficiency resulting in lower operating costs through improved fuel efficiency and reduced maintenance and manning costs.

b) Technical harmonization and standardization A mutual recognition within the community of the technical equipment of ships is being considered by the Commission. Previously costs have been high in transferring vessels between community ship registers because of the need to change equipment completely, carry out supplementary work to existing equipment, and additional testing, and because of the time in delays.

The single market has given much impetus to this work. Technical obstacles should not be a hindrance when transferring ships between community shipowners and member states' flags with regard to the community ship register.

c) Social measures In consultation with the Joint Committee on Maritime Transport, the Commission hoped to develop measures relating to:

- the improvement of working conditions in the shipping industry;
- the drawing up of common programmes of training and retraining to coincide with the needs for technological change;
- the mutual recognition of diplomas, licenses and certificates of competence.

d) Ensuring the observation of international IMO/ILO standards By ensuring the observation of the IMO and ILO standards on safety of ships and crew and for protection of the environment, the community fleet can benefit through eliminating unfair competition from ships not observing those standards.

e) Promotion of community flag shipping in transportation of food aid The Commission believes that the transportation of community food aid - surplus food which is exported - should be done by ships flying the community flag, whereas previously vessels flying a wide range of flags were used.

f) Definition of a community shipowner This is important particularly regarding the transportation of food aid and because of the removal of cabotage restrictions (discussed below). If community shipowners are going to benefit from such measures, it is evident one must clearly define what an actual community shipowner is.

g) Removal of cabotage restrictions The Commission wishes to remove the restrictions on cabotage.

It is stated that all the countries of the community will open their ports to all other countries of the community, but this will only apply to vessels registered in the community ship register, EUROS.

It would apply to freight transport, passenger transport and offshore work, and the requirement on manning would be the same as in the member state.

EUROS background/initial pressure for flag

The prospect of a European flag, with its twelve gold stars in a circle on a blue background was first raised on 12 July 1988 by the then Transport Commissioner, Stanley Clinton Davis, and interest was created in the European Parliament thanks to a report in July 1988 for the European Parliament Transport Committee from the West German Euro MP, Manfred Ebel. Ebel wanted to see the European flag emerge in order to help the region's ailing shipping sector.

He said that so far shipping companies had been able to survive against the competitive advantages of foreign lines by specialization and flagging out but that, on average, over the last two years two ships a day had been changed from an EEC flag to that of another state to enjoy lower costs.

Ebel also listed several areas in which he felt that EEC shipping had a positive influence:

- cross trading which generates billions of dollars a year;
- the region's merchant fleet saves exporters between $4 billion and $5 billion each year in foreign exchange outflows because of the trade it carries;
- by maintaining a significant fleet the EEC can maintain influence over general conditions governing international sea transport;
- can continue to play a part in negotiations on access to cargoes, tariff formation, technical standards and environmental protection.

The notion of an 'Euro flag' was therefore attracting a number of adherents; even shipowning groups sounded encouraging but here was where considerable problems also lay.

To begin with it would appear necessary that such a register be used only to supplement national registers rather than replace them; if this was the case however, what possible incentive would an owner have for incurring the extra costs of an additional flag? To make any sort of sense a European flag must have more than symbolic value. A vital question to be asked is whether 'EUROS' could be made attractive enough to dispense with the need for a second, or offshore, register (shipowners wanted EUROS to contain all the advantages of an offshore register)? Also, would it be possible to link community aid proposals with membership of an European register so that there was a real incentive to fly the European flag?

Financial questions were no less divisive - some states were already pressing ahead with measures to reduce direct taxation of their seafarers, and ameliorate social security costs. This created envy among some not so fortunate, while others had suggested such assistance was unfair, in some way against the spirit of the Treaty of Rome. Other governments had made it quite clear that the singling out of a small group of workers for special taxation treatment was quite out of the question.

There seemed little chance of a consensus : Italy, Spain and Portugal would always prefer subsidy to a special tax regime; France, the Netherlands, Denmark and Germany leaned towards taxation and social security assistance; and the UK (and others) remained opposed to special cases. It would appear that if there was to be a compromise it should keep well away from any sort of blanket approval for fiscal help.

It was left therefore to Karel van Miert (the newly appointed European Commissioner for Transport) to come up with a package of measures to promote the community's shipping fleet while reconciling this with EEC rules on competition; out of this came the proposed single European register, EUROS, with the terms and conditions it was to be operated under.

Initial proposal for a community ship register

The Commission of the European Communities in their publication of 3 August 1989, put forward the possibility of setting up an EC register (whose ships would fly the community flag) as a further measure to stem the decline of the community fleet.

While the single community register conception could not be seen as a short term prospect, the establishment of a parallel register would be technically and legally feasible, the Commission believed. Ships would remain on the register of a member state under this arrangement and would remain under the control and jurisdiction of the member state. However, they would also be eligible for registration in the community register, subject to certain conditions intended to ensure that the register serves its purpose of contributing to the maintenance of a community shipping fleet and a workforce of high quality community seafarers.

Single community register

There are obvious attractions in the establishment of a quality and competitive single community register, but the legal and practical implications would need careful examination.

Existing maritime law and conventions vest jurisdiction and control in administrative, technical and social matters in the national state. Administrative needs include a competent inspectorate to secure compliance with international conventions and enquire into maritime casualties. There are also policing and legal functions which can include detection and dealing with fraud and the arrest and enforced sale of vessels if necessary.

The community could play a fuller role in the international maritime organisations dealing with the technical and social aspects of shipping; in time it could accede to IMO and ILO conventions and accept certain responsibilities but this would first require amendment of those conventions to make community accession possible.

Parallel register

Alternatively the Commission put forward the setting up of a parallel register to member state registers. As mentioned beforehand, vessels will be registered in a national ship register of a member state and, while staying in that register, would also be eligible to register in the community register providing adequate safety and social standards on board such vessels are being enforced and will be enforced by the member states concerned. Vessels acquired by community vessel owners on the basis of a bareboat charter and entitled to fly the flag of a member state would also be eligible to be registered in EUROS, if the following conditions were fulfilled: (from Annex 1, Article 5).

a) the vessel is registered as a bareboat chartered vessel in a national ship register of a member state;
b) the laws of the vessel's initial flag country allow bareboat registration in another country;
c) the consent of the owner of the vessel and of all mortgage creditors for the registration of the bareboat is obtained and;
d) the bareboat charter is duly recorded in the register of the vessel's initial flag country.

From Annex 1, Article 4, eligible for registration in EUROS is any sea going merchant vessel of at least 500 GRT, built or under construction which is already registered in a member state, if it fulfils the following conditions:

a) the vessel must be and remain registered in the national ship register for the duration of its registration in EUROS;
b) the vessel must be owned and for the duration of its registration in EUROS, remain owned, by a person entitled to register a vessel in EUROS, or operated by a community vessel owner on the basis of a bareboat charter in accordance with the bareboat conditions above;
c) the vessel shall not be more than twenty years old.

The parallel register would set minimum requirements for the conditions regarding the nationality of seafarers and thereby seek to obtain the observance of such requirements throughout the community.

Conditions for registration as a community vessel would include a requirement that at least a specified number or proportion of seafarers on board should be nationals of a member state. Such a condition would place a limit on the number of foreign and non domiciled seafarers who could be employed by community shipowners, and safeguard the employment of a minimum of community nationals employed on board the vessels concerned. Article 7 says that:

On vessels registered in EUROS all officers and at least half of the rest of the crew shall be nationals of a member state.

Owners of ships on the EC register would however have to employ member states' nationals in greater numbers than the specified minimum, where this was a requirement of the member state register involved. Ships on member state registers which permit a lower proportion of member states' nations would be admitted to the EC register only if they complied with or exceeded the EC minimum.

The crew nationality requirements would aim to achieve one of the objectives of the community ship register, which is to secure the employment of European seafarers in highly skilled functions and as far as possible, those in other functions.

The community ship register, while requiring a substantial European element in the manning of the highly skilled functions would not prevent shipowners of ships registered in it from employing third country seafarers at rates agreed with their representative organisation, provided that the provisions of the ILO wages, hours of work, and Manning (Sea) Recommendations (No. 109) of 1958, were respected. Equally, social security for seafarers of third countries must be provided on a level which reflects the standards of the country where the seafarer is resident, following the provisions of the ILO Social Security for Seafarers (Revised) Convention, No. 165.

In determining the minimum employment requirements for the community register, account should also be taken of the differences of operating costs with the community shipowner's major competitors and the need that they be reduced to an acceptable level. This would enable them, together with other competitive advantages to be sufficient to compete effectively in the world market.

The Commission believed then that the flying of the community flag would be an indication that the vessel concerned met high standards of quality, reliability and safety (safety standards would relate to the 1981 principles of the International Maritime Organization rather than to those of the member states involved). Within the EC register, obstacles to the transfer of ships from one member state register to another could also be removed through the recognition of technical equipment (Article 12). Also, the free movement of seafarers between vessels on the EC register would also be facilitated through the mutual recognition of their qualifications (Article 13).

The establishment of a parallel community register is seen by the Commission as having other obvious attractions; the European flag would be a powerful reminder of the community presence in global trade, and a symbol of the community as a single trading entity.

The Commission believed that, technically and legally speaking, the setting up of a parallel register was not a problem; it was not in conflict with the new UN convention on conditions for registration of ships since it did not lead to registration in two different states. The ship remained on its national register and the legislation of the member state governed the control and jurisdiction over the vessel.

Reaction to EUROS

Introduction

The Commission believed that there were definite advantages to be gained by joining the community register. One advantage was that it would make easier the adoption by the individual EEC countries of a coherent system of tax and financial measures which would reduce the cost of the maritime transport sector, while avoiding a distortion of competition within the company. Also they believed it would make easier the transfer of EEC ships from one member country to another without further expense and formalities; the same would go for the transfer of crew between member states and the mutual recognition of seafarers' qualifications.

EUROS claimed, therefore, to have political, financial and practical benefits but given the widely differing philosophies and practices of individual member states, there would appear to be considerable difficulties in reaching a common position; the apparent advantage of being able to shift vessels between member states gave rise to the substantial problem of technical compatibility of equipment between the vessels.

Other drawbacks appeared to be that there was no actual direct fiscal benefit and no real political back up from any of the countries (reinforcing the view that problems would arise when attempting to reconcile the differing requirements and objectives of the European Community countries).

At the end of the day only two major advantages seemed to be on offer to those who signed up to EUROS:

i) The Commission wanted to restrict the transport of food aid - surplus food which is exported - to community ships and vessels from beneficiary countries. Also owners operating ships under the community flag would have access to cabotage, with vessels of less than 6,000 tons.

To prevent shipowners who did not have sufficient links with the community from benefiting unfairly from this assistance, the Commission wrote new rules laying down that a community shipowner must have 'a notable presence' in the community.

ii) The Commission also seemed to be softening its approach to shipping consortia. A prime means of reducing overcosts and running costs of companies' operations has been the increasing tendency to form consortia, of which there are now some forty within European based conferences. They are considered by the industry, as well as by governments and shippers, as being an essential way of rationalizing resources and achieving the advantages of economies of scale as well as being of benefit to the trade as a whole.

Further doubts

The European Community proposals for the European Community ship register, EUROS, were unable to be implemented due to the resistance from member state shipowners over the conditions and requirements involved; a common position was very difficult to achieve. Many amendments were made, including subsidies for modernizing tonnage and for training seafarers, as vessel owners had made it clear that they would not use EUROS under the original conditions. However, a debate by the European Parliament on EUROS and the abolition of restrictions on coastal shipping, scheduled for 12 September 1990, was criticized by shipowners just a week before it was due to take place.

The European Community Shipowners' Association (ECSA) warned that EUROS must do more to help out owner's operating costs and branded it inadequate in several key areas: reduced taxation for seafarers and social security contributions; the employment of non community nationals; and investment incentives. Owners did not believe it went far enough to assist their competitive position, and trades unions believed it opened the door for further cheap labour policies in the industry. Owners were encouraged however, by what they understood was a willingness by the Commission to consider measures promoting community shipping. The General Council of British Shipping (GCBS), for instance, was of the impression that the European Community Commission was feeling its way towards a correct approach, while continuing to urge that 'the twin burdens' of taxation and manning costs be reduced to the levels of competitors based elsewhere.

The owners, as represented in the ECSA, wanted to employ seafarers from outside the community at the wages and conditions obtained in their home countries, what they refer to as 'flexible manning arrangements, taking account of the latest technological developments', also a cut in corporate taxation and reduced taxation for seafarers, as well as generally more favourable taxation policy for the industry, measures to encourage investment in new and secondhand ships, and the abolition of restrictions and duties on ship imports and exports.

The moves concerning non EC wages, flexible manning, and the measures regarding taxation creased much unease among seafarers however, and was exemplified by a comment from the UK based National Union of Seamen (now merged into a new transport union known as RMT).

The NUS said:

> The encouragement given by the Commission to the deliberate recruitment of low wage ratings who would displace member state citizens from their employment is a unique solution to the problems said to be posed by wage costs in the EC shipping industry. Other industries and services in the EC experience similar, if not higher costs, yet there is no talk of introducing low wage doctors, lawyers, train drivers or whatever.

The NUS scorned the ILO;s convention 109, which it believed set minimal working conditions, with a 'disgraceful' minimum wage of $286 per month, and the sanctioning of unlimited working hours.

Plans for the new register were further undermined when the proposed debate on 12 September 1990 was postponed to 13 September 1990 to make way for a debate on the Gulf crisis and was then put off indefinitely after a vote was forced in Strasbourg by Kenneth Stewart, Labour MEP for Merseyside West, which led the matter to be referred back to the assembly's transport committee. Mr Stewart said the proposals were 'contradictory and totally alien to all the members of European seamen's organizations'. He also said that Brussels' proposals amounted to 'a further extension of flags of convenience paid for by the taxpayers of Europe'.

Considerations for the new EC flag, EUROS, were therefore shelved and along with it went the changes in cabotage services. Currently France, Greece, Italy, Spain and Portugal impose restrictions on other trading vessels. The EC Commission had proposed that these restrictions should be lifted and that the services only open to vessels entered in the planned EUROS register. However, conflicting national interests and labour tensions within the community have, for now, put paid to any moves towards a liberal shipping policy.

Recent developments

Recent developments have seen the EC Transport Commissioner, Karel van Miert, attempt to make the proposed EUROS register more competitive. Early in 1991 saw the Commission preparing revised proposals which included setting different standards of crewing for cargo and passenger vessels, introducing a uniform tonnage tax similar to the Greek system, exempting seafarers from income tax and giving direct aid to shipowners under the flag. These new proposals open the door to the increased employment of foreign nationals on EC ships, excluding ferry traffic. Problems are posed, including the lack of funds for aid, and the incompatibility with the fiscal regimes of individual nations, but nevertheless this is a step in the right direction.

The most recent moves occurred in November 1991, when the Commission announced on the eighteenth of that month , that it intended to adopt fresh proposals for EUROS by the end of the year. In particular, these would centre around income tax relief for seafarers employed on EUROS flagged vessels with the other EUROS concepts remaining unchanged. The immediate response by the European Community Shipowners Association (ECSA) was that more was needed - particularly relating to flexible manning. Discussion continued on 17 December 1991, in a meeting of transport ministers who, in the words of van Miert, welcomed the latest proposals. At the time of writing we await results of further discussions.

Conclusions

It would appear then that the original concept for a community flag is doomed to failure, or certainly modification. Certainly the notion was a worthy one; the steady rise of the open registry fleets contrasted sharply with the even greater decline of the community fleet and measures were indeed necessary to arrest the increasing tendency of shipowners operating under their national registers to transfer their vessels to open registers outside the community. However, the implementation was to prove more difficult.

The community, with its theme of 'liberalization and harmonization; at the forefront of any policy, attempted to assist the community fleet with a number of proposals, one of which was the proposed European flag, EUROS, designed to run in parallel with national registers. The benefits the community believed would accrue to the community shipowner if he signed up to the flag however were not apparent to the shipowners themselves. They had previously stated that they required the proposed register to contain all the advantages of an offshore register and this it certainly did not.

Even some of the supposed benefits were found wanting. It was stated that vessels would be able to be shifted between member states with ease but this gave rise to the problem of technical compatibility whereby vessels of different states use different technical equipment on board thus making transfer of the vessels very difficult.

Also EUROS vessels were, once cabotage restrictions had been lifted, to be the only users of these services. However, conflict among those nations who were unwilling to lift their cabotage restrictions meant a further benefit of the proposed European flag was lost.

Though amendments were made in an attempt to reconcile the shipowners to the proposal it was clear that from the owners point of view, common ground would never be reached. Having 'tasted the fruits' of open and offshore registry with their lower (or sometimes non existent in the case of taxation) operating costs and having enjoyed lower crewing costs by being free to employ non EC nationals at reduced rates compared to their EC counterparts, owners' requirements were never going to be matched by the EUROS proposals.

Indeed, the UK's House of Lords Select Committee on the European Communities, said a European flag would 'compound the mischief' of flags of convenience.

The Lords' Committee, in its November 1990 report on community shipping measures, while welcoming some of the EC's measures and recognizing they could emerge in a different form, said of EUROS:

> The committee sees the proposed community ship register as a new kind of flag of convenience, based on its financial attraction rather than its legal responsibility for enforcing standards. A single community flag could have symbolic value but it would be a distraction from the real problems.

EUROS as a challenge to flags of convenience then, is inadequate. Though many of its proposals under which it was to be operated were commendable and are indeed beginning to emerge in a different form in 1992, it is very difficult to impose blanket conditions of operation on member states who all have among them differing philosophies and practices.

References

Branch, A.E. (1989), Elements of Shipping, 6th Edition, Chapman and Hall.

Bredimas, A.E. and Tzoannos, J.G. (1981), In search of a common shipping policy for the EC, Journal of Common Market Studies, Volume XX, No. 2.

Chorley and Giles, (1987), Shipping Law, 7th Edition, Pitman Publishing.

Cooper, T. (1989), 'Essential ingredients of a community shipping policy - a shipper's perspective', Seaways, pp. 11-12.

Eliades, Marios, (1989), 'Is there a place for a European flag?', Seaways, p. 3.

Erdmenger, J. (1988), International Symposium on Liner Shipping IV, Conference Report, Bremen.

Erdmenter, J. and Stasinopoulos (1988), The shipping Policy of the European Community, Journal of Transport Economic and Policy, Vol. XXII, No. 3, pp. 355-360.

Fairplay (1991), 'EUROS register proposals revised'.

Hackett, B. (1987), 'Newly Emerging Registers', Lloyds Maritime Information Services.

Jacobs, J.H.G. (1989), Creating Freedom of Maritime Trade in Europe; the next vital steps to complete the single market. National Waterways Transport Association Conference - Short Sea Europe, Paper 1, London.

Lacalamita, M. (1989), 'Essential Ingredients of a Community Shipping Policy - shipowner's perspective', Seaways, pp. 10-11.

Lasok, D. and Bridge, J.W. (1987), Law and Institutions of the European Communities, Fourth Edition, Butterworths.

Marine Engineering Review, (1985), 'Is there a future for the European Shipowner?'

Telegraph, (April 1990), 'What's in store for you in 1992', pp. 8-9.

Which Register? Which Flag? Conference, (1987), Lloyds of London Press Ltd.

Whitelegg, J. (1988), Transport Policy in the EEC, Routledge.